UX Management Methods:

A User Experience Design Leadership Guide for Beginners

How to Lead UX Designers or Master the UX Research Lifecycle as A Team of One

Written By Jon Binder

Also by Jon Binder

UX Research Methods

UX Design Methods

UX Writing Methods

First paperback edition: October, 2021

Cover Design by Rica Cabrex

Edited by Kiara Jackson

Special Thanks to Jonathan Weirich, Esq.

Paperback ISBN: 9798499146712

Hardcover ISBN: 9798750123247

Table of Contents

"Most people make the mistake of thinking design is what a product looks like.

People think it's this veneer—that the designers are handed this box and told, "Make it look good!" That's not what we think design is.

It's not just what it looks like and feels like. Design is how it works."

—Steve Jobs, 2003

New York Times interview

Preface:

UX Management Methods is a guide for how to lead your UX team to greatness. Learn proven methods for hiring, managing, motivating, and aligning your UX team. Use these insights to hire the best UX unicorns, focus your team with a roadmap of key UX deliverables, and measure your team's success and ROI with analytics. A game-changer for anyone leading or working in a team of UX designers or researchers.

Written by Jon Binder, an MIT-trained User Experience Researcher with a Master's degree in Human-Computer Interaction (HCI) and UX Manager with over 20 years of leading and working with diverse technology teams.

Learn how to perfect the art of management while also lifting your team's spirit and tackling the demands of UX to produce the best experiences.

Streamline your UX Operations with proven methods and processes that you can follow to deliver projects on time and under budget. Plus, a detailed Q&A section provides answers to the most frequently asked UX Management related questions.

If you want to sharpen your user experience leadership skills and build a strong team of talented experts, then start learning UX management today.

Introduction

The UX industry is booming. Every day, thousands of large organizations and small businesses alike are struggling to build and grow their user experience teams.

Today, User Experience is no longer just about making your website or app look cool - it's about making your organization more effective, competitive, and compassionate in the digital age. It's about intimately understanding who your users are and what they really care about so that you can provide the best possible experience and meet their needs better than anyone else.

User experience (UX) is how someone interacts with and experiences an organization's products, services or systems. It includes the user's perception of ease of use and the product's ability to deliver value by accomplishing a task or solving a problem. Although user experience is subjective, the principles that make up the user experience are objective.

Since we know the success of an organization is directly related to the quality of the experiences it provides to its users, UX Managers are crucial to the overall success of any business or non-profit.

And there's a good reason that over the years, user experience has become one of the most sought-after careers. Tech industry leaders understand that delivering a superior customer experience not only sets them apart from the crowd but also can deliver huge shareholder returns.

The success of stand out companies such as Tesla, Apple, AirBnB and Amazon can in large part be attributed to delivering an outstanding customer experience. In fact, Amazon's vision statement is to be earth's most customer-centric company. AirBnB's founder, Joe Gebbia mainly attributes the UX design and usability of their product with their incredible growth and the current $100 billion valuation of their company. Apple was founded in a culture of delivering great experiences and elegant designs. And Tesla is the fastest growing car manufacturer in the world and spends $0 on advertising, instead directing those marketing dollars into improving the customer experience.

And many older legacy companies are also beginning to understand the powerful impact of User Experience. Wal-Mart's online division saw a traffic increase of more than 200% after they redesigned the UX of their website. These improvements to the user experience can be directly measured on the company's bottom line.

Over the years, UX has become one of the most sought-after roles in tech. Every successful CEO and technology leader understands the value and competitive advantage of delivering a superior customer experience.

During this time of incredible change and technological disruption, the need for UX professionals and UX managers is greater than ever before.

My name is Jon Binder and I love User Experience. I hold a Master's of Science degree in Human-Computer Interaction and an Executive Degree in Operations and Value

Chain Management from MIT. I also hold dual undergraduate degrees in Business Management and International Business with a minor in Economics.

I started my UX career over 20 years ago designing and developing websites for small businesses and individual clients. Back then we didn't call it UX, we simply called it graphic design or human factors.

Today it isn't good enough to simply build a cookie-cutter app or a website. To stay competitive, your user experience needs to be cutting-edge and exceptional. You need to be able to anticipate your customer's needs and deliver more value, faster and better than anyone else.

UX has certainly come a long way since its early days. From the time it was first recognized as a separate field in 1990, UX has become one of the most important parts of any organization's marketing and development strategy.

UX managers have to be more than just talented designers, they must also possess the leadership skills to effectively guide and motivate their teams to find innovative design solutions.

UX professionals with strong design and leadership skills are needed to fill the growing number of managerial roles within all kinds of organizations like universities, state and local governments, nonprofits and startup businesses.

If you read through a job listing for a UX Manager role, you will see that most of the key qualifications revolve around someone who can not only organize UX projects and deliverables but also manage the business side and other issues of the UX team. This is because today's UX managers must work closely with many different internal and external stakeholders to help their organizations succeed.

Successful UX managers know how to lead and inspire their design and research teams while keeping morale high while delivering great experiences through a strong UX culture.

Recently, I've been working in Baltimore, Maryland where I serve as Director of Operations and Human-Centered Design for the Medicaid and CHIP Financial system or MACFin. MACFin is an online cloud-based system that processes Medicaid reimbursements for over 80 million low-income Americans in all 50 US states and 5 U.S. territories totaling over $550 billion each year. Our user base is diverse and vast and it's an incredibly operationally intensive product with regular releases and upgrades using Lean and Agile development methods. Later, we'll discuss more about what Lean UX is, and how Lean manufacturing and Agile development methods grew to become so popular in software development today.

I also co-lead our UX Community of Practice where over 90 UX designers and researchers gather to share insights, crack jokes and discuss all things UX and human-centered design. In later chapters, we'll discuss the importance of creating UX gatherings and meetings centered on building your organization's UX culture.

While researching user experience at the MIT Design Lab, I stumbled upon some amazing methods and techniques that changed the way I approach design. We'll discuss how these methods can be used to lead successful UX teams.

Over the years, I noticed that successful UX managers had certain traits in common, especially in leadership, communication, and project organization skills. I discovered that great UX managers often shared certain distinct leadership traits. By learning how to build your skills in these areas, you can help pave the way for your team to achieve success while harnessing the benefits of user-centered design.

I interviewed many of my heroes in the UX industry as well as peers who had been extremely successful as managers and tech leads. In addition, I spoke with several UX leaders who had been able to successfully grow their teams from just a budding idea or concept all the way into mature UX design teams using processes that worked.

In this book we will discuss:

- How to build an effective UX team that delivers great experiences through end-to-end consensus with your entire organization;
- How to develop a UX strategy that aligns your UX team with your organization's business objectives;
- How to empower your remote UX teams to deliver great experiences without micromanaging them on a day-to-day basis;
- How to keep morale high through regular feedback, open communication, and ongoing recognition of everyone's contributions;
- How to eliminate time wasted on non-value-added activities;
- How to develop a comprehensive UX research plan that will exceed stakeholder expectations; and

- how to measure the return on investment or ROI of your UX activities.

We'll also address some of the most common issues that are encountered by UX managers in their everyday roles, like:

- Lack of end-to-end consensus and agreement on the UX Research and Design process.
- Confusion about roles and responsibilities
- Low morale within the UX team due to poor communication, siloed responsibilities or unclear expectations
- Unrealistic deadlines and heavy workloads leading to increased stress and burnout
- And lack of collaboration and feedback from clients or between departments

While these are just a few of the challenges that we face as UX leaders, there are some relatively simple solutions for how to address these challenges.

The management side of UX is full of opportunities, but also comes with a few landmines to avoid. UX Managers must understand how to motivate their staff and keep them productive while maintaining a fun and enjoyable workplace. [or "while keeping the process (vague) fun and enjoyable]..

Guidelines for UX processes can be vague, and projects can change over time or develop scope-creep, which forces UX professionals to think on their feet and adapt to these evolving needs. Scope-creep is when a customer or manager changes project goals or requirements after the project has already started, and thus increases the size, scale and scope of the project leading to time delays and cost overruns. Scope-Creep should be avoided if possible, and if new areas for improvement are identified while conducting UX research, then separate projects should be formed to address those issues.

The UX industry struggles with a lack of standardization in processes, deliverables, and research methods. Every UX team is different. There are no "standard UX practices" that you can follow to ensure success.

As a result, UX managers often struggle to learn the secrets of what it takes to be successful through trial and error. They spend countless hours learning about their products, users, best practices, and how to manage. This leaves little time to implement the strategies that will help them become great UX leaders.

In addition, there is no standardized [standard? Predefined?]UX career path, and many times job advancement or progression is unclear. UX Designers must also sometimes be researchers, writers, and testers. UX is a very broad topic, with many areas of specialization - each requiring years of training and experience to master.

For example, UX Researchers need to understand human psychology, sociology and cognitive psychological biases so they can gather accurate research and avoid inadvertently influencing participant responses. They need to learn when to apply each research method at the correct phase of the product development lifecycle and how to collect, analyze, synthesize and present actionable findings and take-aways to the project's stakeholders.

To make matters worse, it can be hard to accurately measure the "ROI" or return on investment of your UX investments,and it's even harder to build a strong UX culture within your organization when you're leading and managing a diverse team of UX professionals working either remotely or in the office.

Fortunately, these obstacles can be overcome by using the correct techniques and UX methods, and understanding how the best UX managers think about their job duties and responsibilities.

This book aims to help UX professionals navigate the industry and conduct better UX research and Design. Through a combination of industry best practices, personal strategies, and tips his book is designed for both experienced professionals looking to boost their UX management skills, as well as entry-level designers looking to elevate their careers one day into UX leadership.

How exactly do you become a great UX manager? What are the secrets of success? And what is involved in leading a UX team? This book focuses on these questions.

UX management takes hard work, time, and dedication—just like everything else in life that's worth pursuing. If you're ready to take the next step into UX leadership, then this book is for you!

The question then becomes: How exactly do you become not just an OK or an average manager, but how do you become a great UX manager? What are the secrets of success? And what is involved in leading a UX team? This book focuses on these questions.

After we finish you'll understand the different career specialties within the UX field, some of the challenges and opportunities in working with UX teams, and the importance of having a standardized UX process to organize and streamline your work.

It takes a high degree of understanding about how best to manage UX professionals, knowing what skills you need to make your UX team successful and develop the cultural attributes that push these teams over the edge from good to great

This book will give you an in-depth look into all things user experience it will show you what differentiates good UX teams

And did I mention that one of the best parts about the UX manager's job is that it's not going away anytime soon. The scope of UX and the number of job openings continue to grow every year. So sit back, relax and enjoy the ride.

Chapter 1
What All Great UX Managers Have in Common

The purpose and heart of UX is to deliver great experiences to everyone who encounters our organization's products and services. Every economy is made up of products and services that meet some person's needs.

UX design is the process of crafting an experience that will deliver the maximum amount of value to the maximum number of people while using the minimum required resources.

Creating positive user experiences that provide real value and solve real-world problems is at the heart of what we do.

By this definition, UX can be applied to any type of product or service where the experience is subjective. From flying in an airplane to buying a car, to swiping left and right on a dating app, experiences are all around us.

UX design can be applied to any type of product, service or interaction where the experience can either be enhanced or degraded by changing it in some way.

UX can be used by anyone: bankers, police officers, teachers and even for interactions between countries. Anywhere a person is having an experience, there's an opportunity to improve that experience in some way, big or small.

User Experience is subjective and people can have such different experiences with the same products or services because no two people are exactly alike. Everyone has different values, goals, behavior, upbringing, life experiences, and different parents.

People have different taste buds, different personalities and there exists tremendous variation in preference and taste. Nature seems to love variety, diversity, and change, and with that variation comes individual preferences in almost everything.

People have favorite movies, favorite games, favorite foods, favorite songs, favorite books, favorite sports teams and favorite colors.

On the other hand, people have different pet peeves and things that they hate. For example, some people hate cats, red wine or fresh sushi, while other people like me may enjoy all 3 of these things.

UX design is about solving the problems that matter to the people you are designing for— delivering what's important to them at that time.

UX designers couldn't care less about things that don't affect people or don't matter to them, because that's not useful in creating a great experience for them.

Because of this natural variation, there can be cases where two or more people can have wildly different experiences, even though they're using the same product or service.

UX design is subjective by its very nature, not objective like math equations that always return the same answer when you input the same numbers. Understanding how your target audience perceives value is crucial to provide them with products and services that truly fulfill their needs.

Lean UX seeks to eliminate waste and benefit from the lessons learned from Lean manufacturing. In Lean manufacturing, all value is defined by your customer, and all waste is defined by anything that doesn't in some way improve your product or service in the eyes of your customer.

For example, a car manufacturer may add an extra bolt or another part to an car, but that part is only valuable if the customer experiences it positively and it values it in some way. If the customer doesn't like the extra part or if the part doesn't in some way add to the quality or value in the eyes of the customer buying that car, then that extra part should be considered waste and eliminated altogether.

In Lean manufacturing, there are 7 different kinds of waste, or "Muda" as they call it in Japanese.

Under the Lean system, seven wastes are identified as:

1: Overproduction by creating too much of something.

2: Inventory wasted storage by maintaining a large stockpile.

3: Wasted motion where you don't accomplish a task in an efficient manner.

4: Defects where you don't produce the desired output from a process.

5: Over-processing where you have extra steps in your production that don't improve the value.

6: Waiting where workers or customers have to wait for something to be delivered or work to be completed.

7: Transport where you're shipping or moving something more than necessary.

UX Managers should understand these 7 different kinds of waste and avoid them to create the best experiences possible for customers.

After you begin to practice Lean UX and familiarize yourself with the various kinds of waste, you'll notice them showing up in all different areas of your organization. By being able to recognize when value isn't being provided to your users, you can be in a better position to change your processes to eliminate waste.

If the work being done doesn't benefit or add to the user's experience in some way, then it is a waste and should be eliminated or changed so that it does add value.

Lean UX is the process of eliminating waste and making sure that customer needs are fulfilled with your product or service.

There are many different opinions about what Lean UX is, but I like to think of it as an agile UX approach focused on continuously iterating the design process so that you're continually converging on better ideas. You continually elicit feedback and refine your design until you eventually reach a nirvana of peak customer experience.

Every year, thousands of organizations spend millions of dollars on secret shoppers and UX researchers who go into stores and record their experiences.

Companies like Target, Hilton Hotels and Airbnb pay these secret shoppers to go out in the world and make notes on their experiences, what they like, what they don't like, what they want to see, what they don't want to see, where they have trouble getting help, where it's easy to get help, what problems occur, and more.

These secret shoppers provide companies with priceless information about their customer's experiences and provide them with actionable feedback to improve their operations. They can tweak policies and procedures, retrain or upskill their employees, or provide new products or services to better meet their user's needs.

Every year more organizations are finding value in UX research and design and are hiring UX teams to uncover and better understand their users and products.

Over the years I've encountered many great us leaders and I noticed that great UX managers share the following 7 characteristics:

1) Great UX Managers are Authentic

Great UX Managers understand the importance of being candid and honest during the UX design process. This candidness can and will require providing negative feedback at times, and it is important for Managers to express their feedback in a way that doesn't offend or embarrass their team. One way to accomplish this is by practicing 3rd party disagreement—framing negative feedback from a third person perspective. By saying something like, "Well what do you think the user would think about this feature?" or , "This feature may not bother most people, but there may be some people who are extra picky and this could bother them a lot," you can avoid unnecessary conflict and redirect frustration without making things personal.

2) Great UX Managers are Passionate About People

You need to sincerely care about the people who use your product and empathize with them to deliver the best value.

The reason for this is simple: if you really care about people you'll find it easier to put yourself in their shoes and empathize with them to better understand what they need and want.

If you don't care about your user, then you won't go to much trouble to understand what they want or desire.

Someone may care only so much that you can make a profit from caring but not more. Your competitor, however, may care a whole lot more about the people who use their product, and they're going to do a better job of creating a fantastic experience for them because they understand them better and want to help them achieve their goals.

Great UX managers know that it takes more than just an understanding of UX design to be able to lead a thriving UX team at your company, you need to understand how people's emotions and psychology work to identify their needs.

3) Great UX managers set clear expectations and objectives for their team

Great UX Managers define realistic expectations and understand that it's not always possible to get EVERYTHING accomplished as planned, but the act of creating a plan helps to focus and align the team.

Creating a plan also helps to assign clear roles and responsibilities to team members and encourages accountability.

4) Great UX Managers Build and Grow the UX Culture

Instead of encouraging your employees to compete against each other for advancement or rewards, get them involved in building something together which will be helpful for everyone.

Get your employees involved by forming a UX community of practice, sponsoring a local meetup group or hosting a speaker series..

Forming a strong UX culture internally is not just beneficial for delivering a great product, it also helps to build a better company from within. Your team members will also feel more connected with other departments as they meet different people who are interested in UX.

A UX manager needs to provide guidance to their team to successfully meet these objectives, as building a community focused UX culture will help team members network and learn UX best practices from other professionals in the industry.

Some companies may be reluctant to invest time and money in a UX retreat but the long-term benefits of doing this outweigh the upfront cost.

5) Great UX managers build relationships with their stakeholders

Great UX managers know that they need to keep both their users and business stakeholders in mind throughout the design process.

You need to be able to use both sides of your brain where one side is thinking, "How can we maximize the value that the organization provides?"

And the other side is thinking, "How can we maximize the value and experience for the customer?"

In their mind, one side should be thinking, "How can we maximize the value that the organization provides?" while the side thinks "How can we maximize the value and experience for the customer?"

While business stakeholders and executives also need to understand these parallel goals, UX managers know how important it is to build strong relationships with their stakeholders to get buy-in when you need it during a project.

Sometimes the needs of the users and business goals conflict. A good example of this would be Facebook, where they make more money from ad sales when people spend more time interacting with their products like Instagram and Messenger. However, research data is clear that the more time people spend on Facebook and Instagram the less happy and fulfilled they are with their lives.

This conflict of interest should be avoided by UX professionals, and win-win relationships should be sought after instead. After all, do you want to be the UX designer for a cigarette manufacturer? I'm sure they employ UX professionals, but I personally would decline to make people's experience better in the short-term by getting them addicted to a product or service that in the long-term makes their lives worse.

6) Great UX Managers Value of Analytics and Metrics

Analytics are raw numbers and data to back up your UX research and design. For example, how many more or fewer people are clicking through after you changed the design of your opt-in form? How does the color, font or text size influence the user's experience?

UX managers use different tools to measure their solutions. For example, you can use Google Analytics, Crazy Egg, or KISSmetrics to generate reports on how people are using your website or web application. Using these insights will help UX managers justify design decisions and make data-driven decisions rather than subjective ones.

7) Great UX managers are Strong
Communicators.

Great UX managers are strong communicators
with their teams, stakeholders, and users.
Experience varies greatly within the industry,
and outside of it few people may be acquainted
with even the basics of UX design. A great UX
manager should be able to communicate their
vision and expectations regardless of the
audience.

Here are some tips that have helped me to
become a better communicator at work:

1. Join a local Toastmasters Chapter.
   Toastmasters helps people learn
   how to deliver presentations and
   speak in front of groups of people
2. Watch TED talks on YouTube about
   various communication styles
3. Read blogs about communication,
   storytelling, and leadership
4. Learn how to tell a great story by
   reading books that teach storytelling
   like Made to Stick or The Story
   Factor

I have learned that being a better communicator makes my job easier because it enables me to explain complex ideas to stakeholders and colleagues.

UX managers who can clearly articulate their vision and communicate their ideas with stakeholders will also be able to unify their teams around the task at hand.

Great UX managers always ask for feedback. They are constantly soliciting the opinions of their stakeholders, team members, and users to get a better understanding of what everyone thinks. They never think they know it all or even know the best way to do things, the customer is always right and it's our job to uncover what they want.

UX managers should resist the instinct to make all the decisions and run with them, because in reality, it's very important to collaborate and ask for feedback from those around you.

Every successful organization is built around providing users with a positive experience through either producing products or through providing services. These products and services can take many forms in our everyday lives, but they all exist to provide some sort of value.

Regardless of the products you're working with, the first step is to identify user needs and pain-points. Pain-points are any friction or roadblocks or challenges your users may encounter when they're trying to complete a task or when interacting with your organization. What do your users care about? With this information, you can begin the process of understanding solutions through user-centered development (UCD).

UX Managers can come from many different backgrounds, such as graphic design, business administration and even one of the many social sciences like psychology or sociology. Most people who excel in the field of UX also have a background in technology that helps them translate user needs into well-defined features.

It's not uncommon for someone with excellent project management skills to be hired as a UX Manager, or for someone who excels on the UX and design side to move up into a management role.

To expand the quality and quantity of UX work you need to hire. To hire successfully, you need to hire the best UX people for the job. To attract the best people, you need to communicate what your UX role entails to let the candidates whether their talents and skills would make them a good fit.

UX Managers also need to be able to set milestones, deadlines, team meeting agendas, and follow up with stakeholders on the progress of various projects.

Instead of working alone on UX, or trying to come up with a new UX process for every project, I now have a great UX team who all understand their roles and responsibilities and how their UX work fits into the larger picture. They now handle most of the heavy lifting and we follow a standardized and documented UX process. We'll discuss in a later chapter the benefits of having a standardized UX process and defining team roles and responsibilities.

UX is all about understanding how users feel when they use your product or service, and enhancing customer satisfaction and loyalty by improving the usability, ease of use, and pleasure provided in the interaction between the user and the product.

As new technology becomes available, UX Managers must embrace it and find ways to use it in their work. At the same time, UX Managers must also be able to spot when an emerging technology is just a fad and not worth investing in.

UX managers need to strengthen the team by making sure that everyone is aligned on what they are working on and what they should work on next. Focus the team by setting clear goals and priorities.

We need to motivate and encourage others on the UX creative team to produce their best work while ensuring that projects come in on time and on budget.

A good UX manager needs to be able to operate independently and have strong communication abilities, but a great UX manager also shares the complete UX ethos: advocacy for the user and excellent design.

The role of a UX Manager is nuanced and challenging, but also rewarding. UX Managers get the privilege to take part in a pivotal point in history, where technology is shaping the present and future generations' lives. We advocate for users to help our organizations empathize with and build a more human-centered world.

UX is not really about design at all; it's about people. It's about making people's lives better with improved technology and more inclusive and effective experiences.

A great UX manager's goal in implementing this vision of UX is to motivate, inspire, lead by example, build strong positive relationships with team members and maintain high standards while also being approachable and kind-hearted.

Next, we'll discuss how to hire the best people and grow your UX team. If you've enjoyed this book so far, please consider leaving a review on Amazon. Reviews are a great way to spread the word and I greatly appreciate your help.

Chapter 2
How to Hire and Grow the Best UX Team

At the end of the day, every organization is just a collection of people gathered together to provide some sort of value to their customers.

This all starts with hiring talented people, who are passionate about what they do and then giving them the space to do their work.

Great UX managers are mindful of the balance between being a "manager" and being a "leader." Leaders inspire, motivate, and help unite others towards common goals while managers plan, monitor, and control.

The best UX managers lead by doing, they get involved in the front lines and roll up their sleeves. The rest of the team can see how all their efforts contribute to larger goals and to meeting the user's needs.

Hiring is one of the most important things you can do as a UX manager. If you hire the wrong people then your UX department will fail to deliver, no matter how good your skills as a manager are.

Have you ever heard of the expression, "One Bad Apple spoils the whole bunch", well the same is true in UX? One bad hire can negatively impact the culture and morale of your team and make everyone less productive.

Hiring is all about finding great people with lots of potential, and nurturing them to become valuable members of your team. In a way, your role as a UX manager is very much like being a headhunter but instead of recruiting candidates for other companies, you're recruiting for your own UX team. You should always be on the lookout for good UX talent.

To be a good recruiter, you need to know what qualities to look for. A good candidate will not only possess strong technical skills in UX but also will likely have good interpersonal skills.

These "soft skills" are essential because when working in UX, you will encounter all different kinds of personalities they will need to empathize with and design for... potentially difficult people, especially if they are designing for nationwide or international products and services.

The job of UX is to get into the mindset of your users and try to understand where they are coming from. This means UX professionals need strong interpersonal and soft skills to be effective in their roles.

Some other important characteristics of a good UX candidate are that they are humble, teachable, and willing to keep an open mind.

Everyone makes mistakes and humble people understand that it's just part of the learning process. Nobody likes someone with a huge ego, who can never admit that they made a mistake. Don't be that guy! and Don't hire that guy either. Only hire people who can put their egos aside and calmly overcome personal conflicts to create great work for the users who they're serving.

Over the years I've met many great UX managers who grow and unite everyone, but I've also encountered other managers who struggled in their roles and had difficulty forming a cohesive team, and failed to make a positive impact.

I've seen UX managers struggle to hire great talent, struggle to develop their team with training and mentoring, and struggle to grow their own skill sets in leadership and management.

One thing I would caution against in the hiring process is not just hiring people who are similar to you. If there are too many UX members on a team who share the same kinds of backgrounds, personalities, and experiences, then the team will likely struggle with thinking outside the box and coming up with creative solutions to new challenges.

In my experience, UX design teams that are too similar also struggle more with group-think and peer pressure issues. In the struggle to fit in and be accepted, many people put their creativity and best work aside to agree with the group consensus.

One of the best ways to combat dogma and groupthink is to hire UX talent with different backgrounds and perspectives. This helps create a more well-rounded and diverse UX department in terms of natural talents, technical skill sets, problem-solving perspectives, and communication styles.

Steve Jobs had a philosophy when hiring people for Apple that might sound kind of crazy to anyone who hasn't worked in software development before.

Steve noticed that the very best software developers would quite easily be up to 20 or 25 times more productive than just an average software developer at the very top of their field that "A-players" would sometimes be able to produce work that even if you put many average developers together they couldn't saw

Steve explained that in the world of information workers, you could find uniquely talented programmers and software developers who were up to 20 or 25 times more impactful to the organization in moving them ahead towards accomplishing some of the most difficult parts of the project

In speaking with the Sacramento Historical Society, Steve made an analogy to explain this phenomenon. "The very best taxi drivers," Steve said, "are only a few minutes faster to their destinations than average taxi drivers."

But the world of software development benefits from the ability to copy software multiple times and this infinite scaling ability. It costs almost the same amount to produce 1 copy of a new video game, or produce 1 million copies of the game, most of the work goes into the beginning where you create the first copy. After that, it's easy to duplicate that copy after the code is written.

The cost of producing 2 cars is double the cost of producing one car, but an additional unit of software, after the first one is created, is essentially free. It doesn't matter if you copy an application one time for a single user, or one billion times to benefit people all around the world.

Steve Jobs knew this powerful truth and spoke about how Apple focuses intently on hiring only the, "best of the best" or what Steve called "A-players" to join their team.

Even today, in modern times Apple employees have explained that their interview process can take up to 5 months. This ensures that Apple is bringing on only the very best talent. As a UX manager, you probably can't spend 5 months looking for qualified candidates so we're going to talk about some techniques to source quality UX talent, quickly and consistently. However, this mindset of hiring slowly and carefully should be at the forefront of your mind.

Careful hiring is also important because of another phenomenon of self-policing that Steve noticed. He explained that he noticed that once you got a group of these "A-players" together, (5 or 6 to start) it became a self-policing group that didn't want to let in any B-level players or C-level players in. The culture develops so that the team only wants to work with other A-players with who they resonate and connect.

Steve said "The difference between the average programmer and a great one is at least that of 25 to 1. The secret of my success is that we have gone to exceptional lengths to hire the best people in the world. And when you're in a field where the dynamic range is 25 to 1, boy, does it pay off."

Apple was the first company in the world to reach a value above $1 trillion. This extreme market capitalization shows the power of carefully cultivating your talent pool and only hiring the vest best.

There are many ways to approach who you should hire for your UX department, but one thing is certain... if you want to innovate, create products that connect with people and remain competitive in the fast-changing world of technology. Hiring only A-players is a recipe for success.

As a UX Manager, you need to think of your hiring process similar to how Apple would hire any one of their workers. You may not have the large budget that Apple has, but one thing you do have that Apple doesn't is that you're able to focus your attention on 1 or 2 key hires, that if done well, could transform your whole UX Team.

Every hiring process starts with putting together a good job description that explains to the candidates what your organization is and what you do. But, the big difference with good UX job postings is that they focus a lot more on who your users are and what is important to them.

For example, if you represented a retirement community looking for a UX designer to improve their website's ease of use and functionality, you would speak to who your users are, what kinds of tasks are important to them, and what some of the common pain points are.

Seasoned user experience professionals like to see job postings that clearly show who they would be working with and what type of UX designs they could expect to produce.

Today there are two main places where the best UX talent can be found: Indeed and LinkedIn. Indeed.com is an online job portal and job board posting aggregator, and LinkedIn.com is a social networking website focused on career development.

By posting to these 2 places you'll reach most of the qualified UX talent you're looking to hire.

Next, get ready to conduct some interviews. In the job posting itself you should say that the candidate should simply send a copy of your resume along with a summary of why they think they may be a good fit to work with you.

From these submissions, you should review and select a few to reach out and conduct a brief phone interview. It's important to keep it casual for this first meeting.

I can't tell you how many times I have wasted time in a 30 or 45-minute or 1-hour job interview only to have realized in the first 5-10 minutes that this probably wasn't the best job for me and I most likely wouldn't accept the job offer. I've also been on the other end of the table hiring UX designers and researchers, where it's obvious in the first few minutes that the person wasn't a good fit, but had to go through the motions to act interested to be socially polite.

Keep the first round of interviews short and sweet. 10-15 minute phone calls are perfect for this first round of interviews. This can help to quickly weed out anyone who may not be a good match.

In this call, you want to open by finding out more about the candidate's background and what got them started in UX. A good answer to this question may be that they've always been interested in either design or art or in improving people's experiences in some way. A bad answer might be that they don't have a background in design or technology, don't seem very empathetic or caring, and are simply wanting to make a career change and work in tech.

After completing the first round of these phone interviews with several candidates, then you should narrow in on the best 2-3 candidates to schedule a more in-depth 30-45 minute online zoom call to meet the rest of your team.

It's important to get your UX team's buy-in, if you have a team at all, if not that's OK and you should conduct the interview either by yourself or with someone else you trust.

One reason to involve the team if possible is that there's nothing worse for a UX team's culture and morale than when a manager makes a unilateral decision and hires someone who doesn't end up fitting in with the team. This almost always could have been avoided if you take the time to introduce the candidate to the rest of the team and see how they "vibe", or interact with everyone else.

It should go without saying, but good UX talent is scarce. By refreshing your UX job postings from time to time, you can ensure that you're attracting new UX job seekers who could be the best new talent to enhance your UX team.

Technical skills are important, but beyond these technical skillsets, there are also the more "softer", or emotional skills that make up a great UX designer or researcher.

While you're interviewing the candidates you should be thinking about what it would be like working with that person on a day-to-day basis and how they would impact morale, creativity, and the output from your team.

A UX Manager's time is extremely valuable, so hiring candidates in an organized and streamlined manner is critical. The optimal strategy for hiring great UX talent is to begin with a short phone interview, that leads to a longer video interview, that can lead to them meeting and interacting with your team. By spending time only on qualified candidates you can avoid wasting time.

The first step of the hiring process is putting together a good job description that attracts the best possible UX candidates. The job description should be well written, concise, and provide enough information for potential UX applicants to make the best decision about whether or not they would like to apply. The title of the position, company culture, and people that are currently working at your organization can all be very attractive factors in hiring new UX employees.

The next step is creating an application process that is optimized for attracting the best UX applicants. A good UX application should include a simple job description that gives a brief overview of what's required and what you're looking for in new hires, as well as an online form where potential employees can apply and send over their relevant work. The potential UX applicant should also be able to see examples of previous work from your company.

After asking your network for referrals to potential UX employees, the next step is to post your UX job posting to a social and a traditional job board. The most relevant job networking website is LinkedIn. Also, post on a job posting aggregation website like Indeed, which collects posting from all around the internet.

LinkedIn and Indeed are 2 good options because these websites are frequented by the top UX talent and you will be able to tell how many applicants there are for a given role. It's important to "fish where the fish are" and go to the places with the most potential UX applicants if you want to reach out to the best talent.

The next step of the hiring process is 1-on-1 phone interviews and in-person interviews with your UX team. First, do a phone interview with all UX candidates who seem like they may fit in well with what we're looking for, and then narrow it down to the top applicants.

After your phone interview, bring in all of your top UX candidates for an in-person interview with you and members of the UX team.

During the in-person interviews, it's important to ask UX candidates questions that will give you a good idea about how they work on teams, deal with difficult situations, and their ability to communicate ideas. These are all important skills that any great UX team member should have.

Before we discuss the specific interview questions to ask UX candidates, it's important to mention the 7 most important traits and characteristics for UX.

It's important to remember to hire for the intangibles and train for the tangibles. You can always train someone to use a tool or a research method, but it's very difficult to train someone how to be charismatic or how to be empathetic and connect with someone on an emotional level. Some things can't be taught in

school or through a book and can only be
learned naturally or by doing.

Empathetic and Warm

Probably the number 1 most important
attribute to look for in a UX applicant is
empathy. Empathy is the ability to understand
and share the feelings of another. The ability to
imagine how you would feel if you were
another person and to put yourself in their
shoes to understand and relate to what they're
feeling. Not everyone has this ability and
sometimes people who excel in some areas
cannot function properly socially or understand
and accurately perceive what other people are
thinking and feeling.

Any effective UX professional needs to be able
to empathize with their users by being able to
put themselves in different types of users'
shoes depending on the product they are
designing for. The greatest UXers are
compassionate since they can put themselves
in the shoes of users and better understand
their hopes, fears, and desires.

A good interview question to determine if someone is empathetic is to ask them how they feel about one of their favorite products or designs. Ask them, "what are some of your favorite products and brands, and how does the experience make you feel?"

The UX candidate should be able to easily communicate their feelings about the product and describe what they like and why that product or design is so emotionally appealing to them.

Another interview question to ask to determine empathetic ability is if they ever worked on a challenging project that required them better understanding the user's perspective or point of view to answer a design-related challenge or question. The UX candidate should be able to express their history uncovering user desires and connecting the dots between motivations, actions, and outcomes.

By listening to how UX candidates describe their past UX projects and experiences, you can better understand how empathetic they are.

Creative

Creativity is the second most important characteristic to look for in a UX applicant. If you're looking for someone who can design and prototype great user interfaces, then creativity is critical. Be sure that the applicant has both creative thinking skills as well as practical, hands-on problem-solving and design skills.

A good interview question to determine if someone is creative is to ask them if they ever designed anything outside of work and what it was. The UX candidate should be able to describe the project with ease, as well as how they handled any design challenges that came up throughout the process.

Another interview question you can use is asking UX candidates if they worked on a project in which they had to imagine a product or service that doesn't exist yet. The UX candidate should be able to describe what they designed and how they went about solving the various design challenges that came up during this process.

Persistent and Tenacious

Tenacity is the quality or fact of being very determined. Determination is an important character trait not only for UX but for anyone. UX designers need to be persistent because researching and designing can become very difficult at times, especially when working with different screen sizes, resolutions, different operating system constraints, and different user groups.

It's not always easy to stay motivated when you're faced with dozens of technical and personal problems. It's important to find people who won't be discouraged easily and will keep going until the project is complete even if things get tough.

If you're looking for someone tenacious, ask them if there was ever a time when they faced resistance on a project and what they did to successfully overcome this resistance. The candidate should be able to explain how they were able to rise above the challenge and still achieve results.

A creative UX candidate will be able to come up with insightful products and services that do not currently exist; tenacious candidates can solve design problems by sticking to their guns and working through challenges to the end.

Team Player and Collaborative

When it comes to UX work, teamwork is essential and everyone's input is valuable. It's about how well you work together, not what you can do individually that makes a UX team strong.

There's an old parable that says that if you want to go somewhere fast, then go alone. But, if you want to go far, go with others. UX is a marathon and not a Sprint. If you want to be able to create great experiences and designs, then it's going to take time and a lot of work and this can only be accomplished with a focused and effective team.

The ability to work collaboratively and share ideas is a good quality to look for in UX candidates. Look for someone who is unselfish and willing to collaborate on new ideas.

A good interview question to determine if someone is a team player is to ask them if they have an example of a project where they worked on a team and what role they played in the group. The UX candidate should be able to explain their role with ease, along with how they helped contribute to the overall success of the endeavor.

Another good question is to ask them how they would react if their coworker proposed a different design solution to a problem than the one they originally suggested. The UX candidate should be able to explain why they either decided to adapt their solution or push back.

A good candidate will also be able to explain how they contributed to a collaborative UX design project; team players are unselfishly helpful throughout each step of the process, without having to be asked.

A good interview question to determine if someone is collaborative is to ask them about a time when they worked as part of a team. The UX candidate should be able to explain how their role contributed to the overall success of the project, as well as how they worked effectively with others during this project's various stages.

Curious

Curiosity is defined as being eager to know or learn something. A UX professional who is curious is always looking for ways to uncover the answers to questions and improve the UX process. Someone who doesn't like asking questions about why they don't understand something is probably not likely to be a good UX team player.

It's important to find out whether a candidate has a history of learning from their mistakes and making necessary changes on future projects based on what they've learned.

Asking UX candidates how they felt when they didn't understand something is a good way to find out if they will ask questions or just keep their heads down and work on the project. The UX candidate should be able to explain that there's always room for improvement and that it's important to learn from mistakes and fix them for the future.

Another good interview question to ask is, "what's something interesting that you've learned recently? A UX professional with a high degree of curiosity is going to be able to easily come up with something they've learned, even if it doesn't apply directly to UX. Someone who isn't curious is not likely to have a high motivation to stay current on information and mentally venture out to learn new things.

Curiosity is positively correlated with intelligence so you can look at curiosity as a sign of how bright and insightful your applicant may be.

Your team members will need to have the curiosity of a child to stay up-to-date with what's happening in UX design, learn new design tools, new research methods, and other innovations. If you don't have a natural curiosity then you're going to find UX very challenging.

Self-starter

Great UX pros are independent and self-motivated individuals. Make sure that your applicant has a strong work ethic and a natural desire to begin working without being told to start.

Candidates should have their own ideas about what makes a great product or service and how they can improve them. They should also be able to naturally look at a product or service and suggest design tweaks or changes that may improve the form or function.

A good interview question to determine if someone is a self-starter is to ask them about a time when they were able to work independently. The UX candidate should be able to tell you a little bit about how they managed their time and what steps they took to complete the task as efficiently as possible.

Self-starters are remarkably valuable and help to get momentum going on projects. That's important for UX because it means that the UX team is going to come up with more original ideas faster.

Motivated to Learn New Skills

UX is a fast-paced, technology-driven industry, and professionals should constantly be learning new skills and adapting as the industry and project demands change. Investigate potential candidates' willingness to be open to learning new things and if they have any specific ideas on the skills they would like to learn.

A good interview question to determine if someone is motivated to learn new things is to ask, "Do you have any ideas on the skills you'd like to learn in the future?" The UX candidate should be able to explain what new skills they could learn that would help them grow in their career and why they're important to them.

Another good interview question is how long would it take for you to feel comfortable using a new design or research software or technology? The UX candidate should be able to explain how they can learn quickly and can be ready to use new tools within a reasonable amount of time. Be careful if the UX candidate seems unwilling to learn new software or skills because UX is an ever-changing ecosystem.

Design-savvy

As we all know, UX design is much more than creating attractive things. It's also about comprehending how design affects users and their experience with your product or service.

A good interview question to determine if someone is design-savvy is what do you like most about UX? The UX candidate should be able to explain that they enjoy the design process and figuring out how to make something work for users.

Be cautious if the candidate says something that doesn't relate to design and improving users' lives. Sometimes people get caught up in the research methods or design styles and forget what it is we do as UX professionals and that we exist to make people's lives better through great design.

Another good interview question to ask to determine if the applicant has good design sense is do you have any design-related pet peeves with any products or services you think should work better? The UX candidate should be able to explain what bugs or defects exist with certain designs and what they would do to try to improve these designs.

The best people working in UX have many options, so they can afford to be picky. A great UX worker isn't going to just accept any job offer or join any organization. They're going to hold out for a great position with a great organization that aligns with their values.

It's important to hire individuals who can carry a conversation and who get along well with your UX team. If you're able to, you should always have the other members of your team meet the candidate and chat with them.

For UX Managers it's important to hire people who are better than you at what they do. This doesn't necessarily mean they need to be more knowledgeable about every single thing, instead, it means you should look for a UX designer who's better at design or a UX researcher who excels in research and will be a natural fit. These A-players will also inspire your team to grow.

There's nothing worse than getting burned on a bad hire. Even the best UX manager won't be able to change a bad hire if they don't fit the team's culture. If you hire a real dud, they may never integrate and fit in with your team's culture. It could be very disruptive and bad for business and design.

Steve Jobs understood there is a compounding effect that happens when you hire the perfect person for the job who resonates with the mission and goals of the organization. They can amplify your efforts and contribute greatly to your overall culture and team growth. Remember, the very best technology professionals can be up to 25 times as valuable as a mediocre or average worker.

As UX managers it's our role to create a supportive environment filled with talented and passionate UX team members, who can be free to do their best work.

But before conducting any interviews or looking for applicants, UX managers should have a strong understanding of their projects' requirements and timelines. It's also helpful to know what stage the project is in and what challenges or issues have been encountered so far.

This up-front research will help determine how closely a candidate's experience matches your hiring needs for a given project or client. It also makes it easier to compare different candidates' strengths and weaknesses more objectively, rather than being influenced by their personality or presentation style during the interview.

UX Designers are the ones who do the actual design work, but they can't do it alone. UX Designers work with researchers to ensure that their designs are based on actual user feedback. Researchers help designers understand the context for what they're designing, understand who they are designing for, and help them avoid costly mistakes that might alienate their users.

It is important to note that research isn't just about data collection, but also about helping you navigate complicated or potentially controversial issues.

But it's also important to remember that there is no 1-size fits all template for what makes someone great at UX. The truth is, there is so much variation and there are so many different skills involved, that you're never going to meet two UX professionals with the same background or the same approach to their work.

One way to help categorize UX candidates is to divide them into three distinct categories based on their skill sets and style of working.

3 animals that represent the UX categories are unicorns, foxes, and hedgehogs.

UX unicorns are the rarest. Those are the people who know all the UX design and UX research-related skills required to lead a successful project. I'm talking about these people who have Pixel-Perfect prototyping skills, ultimate design sense, and also know which research methods to carry out at which parts of the user-centered design research process these people are extremely hard to find but when you get them, hang on to them and treat them well because they can take your team to the next level.

UX Foxes are somewhat uncommon but are still easier to find than us unicorns UX foxes typically have experience in one or more other aspects of the organization before coming to you. For example, they might have marketing Savvy or maybe they have business development and sales skills these people can help translate their sales or marketing or business sense into the user experience, and that way they're able to cross domains while not quite as rare as unicorns UX foxes are still valuable to the team.

Finally, you have UX hedgehogs. Hedgehogs are those people who are absolute experts in one narrow area. You know the people I'm talking about. The kinds of people who are amazing at designing but never ask them to speak to a client because they're kind of awkward or maybe the people who are great at talking to people and great at conducting user interviews and user research but might not be good at all with back and coding or prototyping or creating mock-ups different people have different skill-sets and hedgehogs are people who narrowly specialized in one field but are very rigid and are unable to perform all of the roles that UX unicorns may be able to perform.

By thinking of UX candidates in these three categories: hedgehogs, foxes, and unicorns, you can now understand how hiring managers think about staffing and balancing the skill sets of their UX teams.

Hiring can, at times, be a difficult process. But the rewards of getting it right are worth the struggle endured finding the perfect candidate.

In the next chapter, we're going to talk about the benefits of following standardized UX processes and how processes can help streamline your work and help your team produce high-quality designs in minimal time.

Chapter 3
Following Standard UX
Processes

If you're feeling stuck in your UX project, it might be time to follow a standardized process. Many different methods can work for you, but there are some benefits of sticking with the tried and true UX research and design processes that have stood the test of time.

When your team is following a standardized UX process, you'll experience some of the following benefits:

- A repeating UX process makes it easier to train new people on the team. It provides a guided structure for new employees to follow, so they can learn how to be effective members of your design team.

An important thing to remember is that not everybody knows what UX design is. People outside of a UX design team have a limited understanding of what UX is and how it applies to the product that they're working on. By having standard UX processes based on industry-accepted best practices, everyone—from the CEO to the marketing team—can be on the same page about what UX is, how it works and why it's important.

- A clearly defined process helps your team members know what to do next. When a new UX design task lands on a member of your team's desk, they'll have a clear idea of what to do and how to proceed. Without a UX process, people might not know what to do next or where they should be at any given time during the design process.

- A clearly defined UX process makes it easier for your team members to take ownership of their tasks and feel accountable for completing them. Much like following a travel itinerary when you go on a trip, having a clear process that everyone knows and understands makes it easier to track your progress as a team.

- A clearly defined UX process reduces the number of mistakes made by your team members. Without knowing what they're supposed to be doing at any time during the design process, people can easily make mistakes that cost the company time and money.

- A clearly defined UX process helps your team members prioritize their tasks. UX designers know that distractions are all around them, so they're constantly doing what they can to reduce the number of "distractions" they encounter daily. But when there isn't a UX process in place, team members might prioritize tasks based on their preferences, which can lead to project delays and missed deadlines.

The benefits of having established UX processes in a place far outweigh the cost and time associated with creating them and training your team members. These additional costs and time expenditures will be offset by the reduced mistakes made by your team, as well as their reduced stress levels.

Having a clearly defined process isn't enough on its own—you also need to know how it can be implemented into your company's workflow and culture. This means you should expect some pushback from people who don't understand the value of UX design processes or who don't understand why they're following the same process over and over.

Most people don't understand or appreciate the value of operational processes, which is why they might need some guidance and education to make sure they understand how important UX processes are for the product. You'll most likely encounter people who resist change, so you'll need to enlist help from managers and executives to get people on board with your new UX processes.

Processes help ensure that your team works to the highest standards of usability by bringing everyone onto the same page about what's supposed to happen at any given phase of the development lifecycle.

When things get difficult and you're in the heat of the moment and the fog of war rolls in, just remember one thing: trust the process.

But first, a disclaimer. The UX processes and methods outlined in this book were not all created by me. Many are based on industry-established best practices, common human-centered design standards, and decades of experience by UX professionals worldwide who have studied these methods and put them to work in many different contexts.

The reason that processes and standard procedures are so important is that they form the foundation for your UX work. And just like every house needs a strong foundation, so does your UX work.

Having common standards help us all work together towards accomplishing our shared goals and keep everyone organized and on track during the ups and downs of the project.

Common processes allow teams to consistently produce high-quality designs in a minimal amount of time and enables research to be done more effectively.

When trying to develop processes and standard procedures, it is important to think about what would be most beneficial for your team to include in them. Some UX processes and methods will work for some teams but not others, so I've found the best way is to apply these flexibly rather than dogmatically.

The first thing to do when beginning the process of developing new processes and standard procedures is to figure out what sort of problems you are trying to solve. What are the pain points that you and your team experience when you sit down to do your UX work?

These problems could be related to things like the quality of your final designs, how long it takes for a project to go from start to finish, or even human resources issues such as discipline clashes between members of a team.

Once you have identified the problems that you and your team face, it is good to think about whether or not there are ways in which you can solve them.

The most important thing with processes and standard procedures is to remember they should be designed for people rather than computers. Processes and standard procedures should support UX professionals and their teams in doing great work, not hinder them with poor design.

One of the most common mistakes that I see when evaluating UX processes and standard procedures is that they are often poorly designed for people. Sometimes they can be clunky or too complicated, or maybe their ranking or organizational scheme doesn't make sense to people who use them daily?

Well-designed UX processes and standard procedures will support your team in doing great work rather than hinder them with poor design.

A UX manager's job is to help their team do whatever they need to implement the UX process and standard procedures so that they can get on with designing great things.

UX processes are usually divided into 2 overarching categories:

1) UX Design Processes

2) UX Research processes

Each process within these two phases has its own set of documents, checklists or templates that help your UX design and research team amplify their abilities. At each phase, there are a series of deliverables that give tangible evidence of all the work being done.

It's important to keep in mind that the standard UX processes and methods required by your UX team will vary across different companies, organizations, and industries. The reason for this is that no two organizations or UX teams are the same - they all have their strengths and weaknesses, challenges and opportunities. One team might need to prioritize user research, while another might be struggling with outdated screen designs. One organization may serve millions of low-income Americans while another may cater only to high net worth, 55+ retirees.

UX processes are not necessarily the same as business processes, although some overlap between the two is inevitable. As a UX Manager, setting up your team's processes and standardized methods of working will be one of your main responsibilities.

When I was working at the U.S. Social Security administration's User Experience Group. The user-centered design services delivery process, or UCD process, was a set of standardized UX processes the organization used to plan and organize every UX-related project.

It consisted of a project overview template that listed key milestones and deliverables, as well as clearly listed who we were designing for and what our expectations were as far as work to be completed and results to be delivered.

The goal also is to create standardized UX processes that enable a UX organization to consistently produce great work regularly, no matter what size or scope of the project they were working on.

Having processes also helps greatly when things get challenging, or there were conflicting opinions between the team or stakeholders about what direction to take research and design activities. During this "Fog of War" that can sometimes take place during projects, people become hurried or stressed and begin making rushed or poor decisions. Before this happens, it's crucial to have an action plan. Having a plan allows teams to better avoid going down a rabbit hole, which can sometimes happen when working on new concepts and designs.

It's important to realize that there is no 1-size fits all approach to creating your UX processes. UX is all about advocating for the user and explaining their point of view to deliver the best overall user experience that your product or services can achieve.

As you begin to document your organization's core UX processes, keep in mind that your UX processes are always evolving. This is part of how you keep them relevant, up-to-date, and the most helpful to the UX design team members who use them day in and day out.

For the UX Research category of your processes, some of the most common UX Research processes are:

1) User Interview Process

The user recruitment and interview process should be documented. From the beginning email used to reach out and request a meeting, all the way through to documenting and storing interview findings should be clearly outlined.

By documenting the interview process your team will know the language you use to schedule participants and the process for collecting data and protecting the privacy and anonymity of your participant.

2) Usability Testing

The usability testing process should be documented to ensure that every UX designer uses the same steps, so you can arrive at similar results no matter which team member conducts the test.

By documenting this process your team will have clear documentation of how many participants are needed, what type of users are appropriate for testing, how long each session will last, and what to do when participants don't show up or arrive late.

3) Survey Process

The survey process should be documented and shared with your team. By doing so you'll ensure that every time you're looking to collect data, via a survey, there's one consistent way of reaching out and consistently responding to the feedback provided by participants.

Your team should be well aware of how to create a survey using Qualtrics, Survey Monkey, Google Forms, or another tool. It's also crucial that the team know who owns each project and when it should be distributed within an organization.

4) Competitive Research Process

The competitive research process should be documented. By doing so, your entire team will know what steps they should take when performing research on competitor products.

Within the UX Design category of processes, some of the most common UX Design processes are:

5) Discovery Process

The discovery process should be documented. From the beginning, when you're preparing to begin designing, to the final artifact that's created to communicate with your team or stakeholders.

By documenting this process, your team will have a clear roadmap of how the research will play out and what activities are needed to reach each milestone.

6) Process for Organizing Design Patterns Library

The process for organizing the design patterns library should be documented. By doing so, every member of the team will know where to go when they're ready to add a new pattern or how to update an existing one.

By having a standardized design library, each team member will be able to easily contribute new patterns or update existing ones.

7) Process for Organizing UX Design Templates

UX templates like user personas, journey maps, and service blueprints should be documented. By doing so, your entire team will know where to go when they're ready to access the latest version of a template and what elements can be edited and which ones need to remain as is.

Templates also help add a layer of order and consistency to your UX deliverables. They promote efficiency and reduce frustration for team members who might be looking to access the same files or produce similar deliverables over and over again.

8) Process for Collaborating with Developers on Design Details

The process of collaborating with developers on design details should be documented.

By documenting this process, your UX team will know how to work with developers when it comes to wireframes and storyboards to make sure that their designs are interpreted correctly in code.

9) Process for Safeguarding Participant Privacy and Personally Identifiable Information

To ensure that you're not jeopardizing your participants' privacy, or worse yet giving access to any sensitive information, the process for safeguarding participant privacy and PII should be documented.

By documenting this process, you'll set clear guidelines for how each UX practitioner should handle personally identifiable information and ensure compliance with all federal laws regarding privacy and data.

10) UX Metrics and Analytics Process

The UX metrics process should be documented. By doing so, the entire team will be on the same page regarding what data is needed for each metric and how to go about collecting it.

The UX metrics you collect might include bounce rates, session duration, page views, or similar traffic-related measurements. They may also include more qualitative measurements like user satisfaction, ease of use, or time spent trying to complete a task.

11) Stakeholder Reporting Process

The stakeholder reporting process should be documented. To ensure that everyone is kept in the loop about the progress being made, it's crucial that each meeting is well-documented and results are easily accessible to all team members.

By documenting this process, you'll set clear guidelines for what information needs to be shared with which types of stakeholders at what point in the project and ensure that all team members prioritize the needs of each stakeholder.

Documenting UX processes doesn't need to be a difficult process itself. You can make use of digital tools like Process Street, which is completely free and provides you with everything you need to create highly detailed checklists for each process in your UX workflow.

There are several steps you can take to ensure that your team has a clear understanding of how the UX process unfolds. You should take the following steps to train and align your team around processes:

Map Out Your UX Process Flowchart

The first step towards getting buy-in from your UX team is to create a detailed, step-by-step UX process flowchart. This will not only help you visualize your workflow in an easy-to-understand way but it'll also allow you to break down each step of the process for your team so that they clearly understand its purpose and how it fits into the bigger UX picture. A great tool for making your UX process flowchart is Gliffy, which allows you to create diagrams and infographics quickly and easily.

Make Your UX Process Flow Chart Accessible

After constructing your UX process flowchart, make it accessible to the rest of the team so that it's easy for everyone to understand. You can do this by chatting it up with your team members individually, posting the flowchart somewhere visible in your workspace, or uploading it to an intranet so that everyone can access it.

Involve Your UX Team

Once you've started to break down each step of the UX process for your team, make sure your UX counterparts are brought on board. By doing so, you'll have full buy-in from your UX team during the planning stages of any project.

Document Your UX Processes

The final step is to document each step of your UX process before a new project or as a refresher if it's been a while since you've completed a workflow for a particular type of project. Ensuring that your UX team is involved in planning sessions for new projects is another crucial step to take to get buy-in from each member. When they feel like their opinions are being heard, UX members will be more likely to give their best efforts. By taking the time to explain each step in detail and break down exactly what your team needs to do, members will be able to easily identify which steps need their attention and how they can contribute to a project's success. Doing this for every type of UX project you plan on completing ensures that each one runs smoothly and is completed within a reasonable time frame.

While these are just a few examples of UX processes, they give a good template for what a UX process should look like. Designing your own UX process is more straightforward than it might seem at first glance. You can use the following sections to create a UX process template:

1) Process name

2) what you're looking to accomplish, the goal

3) who should be performing the process and who is responsible

4) when the process should be used in the project development lifecycle

5) any miscellaneous notes or documentation requirements

6) tools that should be used throughout the process

By creating a UX process template like this it will make it easy for design teams to quickly understand where they should be focusing their efforts and how they should be working together.

In summary, following a standardized process is one of the best ways for an organization to achieve success and repeat its results over and over again.

Processes also help ensure that your UX team is following industry best practices, regardless of what type of projects they are working on or where in the world they're based.

Chapter 4
How to Communicate Effectively with Your UX Team

The key to successful UX management lies in communication. Communication with each other within the UX team and communication with internal and external stakeholders.

As a UX manager, you need to make a deliberate effort to schedule touch-points into your teams day by daily stand-up meetings, or brief touch bases. This helps to create a culture of continuous feedback and communication. This also ensures that all stakeholders are on the same page when it comes to UX priorities and goals.

Feedback can be used for project milestones or completed work. Feedback should only be requested when it's necessary and relevant to a specific person or goal.

While the practice of daily stand-ups is not a new idea, it can help UX managers with staying on top of UX Progress as well as creating a collaborative environment within your team. Setting up these meetings once a day allows members of the team to communicate their work progress, what they are working on, and what they need from others.

If you have a UX team member who is behind on work it's important to address this within the meeting. If there is a tight deadline or if work is continually behind schedule, then this should be the primary focus of the stand-up to discuss how best to work together as a team to work past this challenge. This will allow your team members to get help from others before things get out of hand, resulting in a delay in shipments or missed deadlines.

Be sure to not let the meeting go over the time limit during the daily stand-up. 5 to 10 minutes is all you need for these meetings. Set an alarm or timer if it helps act as a reminder for when the meeting will end. It's important to enforce this time limit to keep these meetings short. Within this five to ten-minute window, discuss your progress, issues, and concerns. These meetings are meant to be quick so that the rest of your team members every day and get everyone focused on the same page.

Trello is a great example of how an online tool can help support daily stand-ups within your UX team. It allows you to create tasks for yourself and others, which can be shared across the team. This is a great way to indicate if you need assistance with something or when you are working on it. No one needs to read through email threads or Slack posts to know what everyone is working on; standing up a board in front of the team that shows all work being performed and planned allows people to ask questions or offer help if needed.

Your team may also benefit from creating a shared Scrum board that has monthly, quarterly, and sprint tasks planned out for each person. This is a great way to indicate deadlines and what needs to be completed in a specific timeframe. You can find free tools if you don't want to make a Scrum board on your own, but many times creating a shared list will work too.

As UX becomes integrated within teams and organizations, it becomes imperative that communication with internal stakeholders is strong. Internal communication goes beyond sharing deliverables or status updates with other UXers or Project Managers. It consists of understanding the company's business objectives, their current issues, and how these roadblocks can affect UX processes.

A simple definition for continuous feedback is "the process of giving and receiving information in an ongoing way." Continuous feedback happens constantly as opposed to once or twice throughout a project.

This constant flow of information helps all parties working on a project to stay up-to-date with the tasks being completed, timelines and deadlines.

Setting up a culture of continuous feedback sets the groundwork for a successful UX team. A UX manager will have greater control throughout their projects by being informed of what his team is up to and a UX professional will be able to better prioritize their tasks and goals by understanding if their efforts are in line with the project's priorities.

When establishing a culture of continuous feedback, UX team members need to understand that this type of communication does not replace formal meetings or one-on-one sessions.

These formal meetings are the UX manager's way to communicate important information about their projects, address issues that may arise, and be open to any questions UX team members might have.

The benefits of establishing a culture of continuous feedback include:

- Having more control over projects
- Keeping stakeholders informed on project status (e.g. d
- Better communication and collaboration between UX te
- A better understanding of UX priorities and goals by all
- Improved productivity within the team as a result of hav project needs.

During our Fail of the Week award ceremony, UX team members share an experience they had that could have been handled better or an experience where their ideas were shut down without any discussion. This type of open discussion has allowed UXers within our organization to be more comfortable with sharing concerns and issues as they arise. It also allows for UX managers to learn what types of conversations are happening around the organization about their UXers' work.

You can also have team members meet with stakeholders regularly so they can establish ongoing dialogue and relationships.

UX managers should not only be facilitating the ongoing feedback process, but they should also receive feedback from their UX team members, peers, and other key stakeholders within their organization. Feedback sessions are a great way for UX managers to get a pulse on what is working and what's not from their team members.

When UX team members understand how important it is to establish a culture of continuous feedback, they are more likely to feel comfortable giving their UX manager feedback and will be more open to hearing suggestions.

The goal for the UX manager is to create a friendly and collaborative environment where everyone can ask questions and be open about what they are working on.

Whenever there is a lack of trust in the team or the UX manager, it is harder to establish a culture of continuous feedback.

When things do go wrong, no matter how small it may seem, the UX team manager needs to set up a time where they can all discuss what happened and how it can be avoided in the future.

Finally, a UX manager must be aware that while promoting a culture of continuous feedback, negative feedback should never be the focus. A UX professional's job is to provide constructive criticism and suggest improvements based on best practices. If team members are always receiving negative feedback about their work or behaviors, they may become defensive which will prevent them from being open to receiving criticism.

You should always lead by praising the good aspects of the UX work before identifying areas that need improvement.

Setting up continuous feedback is not something that happens overnight, there are many steps involved when establishing appropriate communication channels between team members.

Establishing open communication does not end with weekly or even daily meetings, UX managers must be approachable at all times. If you have a lot of UX creatives working in the same space, it may be a good idea to create different zones with specific purposes.

For example, you could create an area where team members can relax and take 5-minute breaks to recharge their batteries without getting too distracted. Then there would be the zone with desks for regular work, another zone for brainstorming sessions or big project meetings, etc. At the end of each day, UX managers should get rid of any clutter on the workspace to keep distractions at bay.

Here are some common prompts to elicit feedback and communication from your team members during meetings:

"What are your thoughts?"

This is a question that UX managers should frequently ask their team members for them to get an idea of what their team members are thinking about certain issues or topics at hand. UX managers should also try asking their UX team members for their opinions on the projects they are working on before making any significant changes to get a sense of what is feasible and what isn't.

"What do you think would be a good solution?"

This is another question that UX managers should frequently ask when trying to find out how their UX team members come up with good design solutions. UX managers should expect a variety of different responses but the best response is one that takes into consideration all factors and constraints relevant to a certain problem or challenge.

"Where do you think we should go from here?"

This last question is one that UX managers can pose at the end of projects or presentations to get feedback from their UX team members on how they like what they see or hear. Team members may identify things that can be improved, or even come up with suggestions for further enhancements.

"What should we do about XYZ?"

UX managers can pose this question at the start of a project as a way to get an idea of what their UX team members think about certain topics or issues. Clients may pose this question to figure out what the risks are for doing something and how they can mitigate these risks.

"What don't we know yet that we should discover?"

This is a good question that UX managers should ask when they want to know what their UX team members think is missing for them to make good project decisions. It could help put things into perspective and provide UX managers with insights they can use to improve their decision-making process.

"What if XYZ happens?"

UX managers should pose this type of question to their team members when they want to get a sense of what would happen in certain scenarios. They can use the information gathered from this type of question to come up with possible alternatives and prepare for any possible outcomes.

"If we do XYZ and it doesn't work, then what else should we try?

The "project" in this question could refer to one specific project or it could refer to all of the projects that are currently being worked on. This is a good way for UX managers to figure out alternative routes and predict certain changes that might affect things down the road and what consequences there would be if they were implemented.

"How do you want to be rewarded?"

Sometimes rewarding people doesn't necessarily mean that money needs to be involved. For example, UX managers could reward their team members by saying "Thank you" and using specific wording for this. Asking this question can give team members a chance to share how they would like things to be done as far as recognition is concerned.

"Is there anything I can do to help you with your career goals?"

If UX managers know what their team members' career goals are, they can help them out by facilitating things behind the scenes. This shows that UX managers have a vested interest in making sure that everyone is happy and fulfilled.

"What is your favorite UX project?"

Asking this type of question gives UX team members the opportunity to voice their opinions about different UX projects, no matter how large or small. It also helps UX managers get a sense of what their team's interests are when it comes to working for various clients.

"How would you describe your work ethic?"

Getting a sense of one's work ethic can ensure that there are no issues with motivation or productivity later on down the line. If UX managers don't ask this type of question at the beginning, they might have to deal with certain issues even if they didn't realize anything was wrong until much further down the line.

"How do you define success?"

This type of question enables UX managers and team members alike to gain a better understanding of what the end goal is for both parties- that way there can be communication between everyone involved.

The first thing is to understand that UX team members need autonomy to be productive. It is the UX team members who know what is important and what isn't, so it doesn't make sense for UX managers to tell them what they need to do all the time and neglect their autonomy.

UX team members should always feel comfortable giving feedback and criticism, and this way problems can be avoided before they start hurting productivity or morale.

UX managers should take all feedback seriously and evaluate it for themselves; even if it turns out that there isn't a problem, after all, at least everyone will know that they tried everything possible to avoid one from arising.

UX managers should become proactive when it comes to UX resources so that everyone can feel comfortable. They need to build an environment in which people are relaxed and do not feel as though they are being neglected or treated unfairly.

The key is to make sure everyone understands what the end goal and vision is and then take steps (and communicate them) towards getting there.

Understanding the workflow and logistics of each individual - along with their needs and wants - will enable all parties involved to give input into how best to improve their daily lives within the workplace environment while still achieving company goals and productivity levels.

The information gathered from this stage should allow for improved future planning, delegation, time management, or more, which in turn can lead to a positive work environment, improved morale among employees, and increased UX team member loyalty.

When communicating with your UX design team, it is important to remember that you should treat everyone as an individual. Every person has a different way he/she likes to receive information so try to learn this beforehand so that it will help you communicate better with the UX design team.

It's important to keep your communication clear and concise so that employees will not get confused with what you are telling them. Avoid using heavy words because some of your team members may misunderstand the message you want to convey so always remember to keep it simple.

In terms of communication within your UX design team, there are certain rules and guidelines all members should follow:

- No interruptions while someone is working on something.

- Use constructive criticism to help each other improve and grow as a UX designer, not as competition.

- Address issues directly with the person who caused concern. For example, if your UX team member consistently focuses too much on their work and doesn't include other team members, then talk to him/her about it.

- Communicate with each other regularly whether it's through meetings or casually talking about projects and concerns to make sure everyone is working well and everything is going as planned.

- During your UX design team meeting, make sure you address issues promptly and give out assignments immediately so that they won't be left hanging.

- Be open to discussions with other team members and address their concerns as well because you want the UX design team to work together especially if they are working on a common project or task.

- Be flexible enough to change your stand, decision or opinion when needed. While compromise is important in a leadership role, it is more important to ensure your UX design team members are on the same page.

- Allow time for creativity during work hours. Don't be too strict with your UX design team because they will end up not wanting to come into work or do extra work outside of work.

- Regularly check in informally with your UX design team to ensure everything is going as planned and schedule meetings for progress reports.

- Hold regular UX design team meetings with team members so that everyone is working well together and no one is stepping on anyone's toes.

- If you notice a member of the UX design team has been distracted or has a lack of interest in their work, talk to them and understand why. Maybe they're not feeling part of the team or have been given too much work to do so help them if you can.

By communicating effectively with your UX team, you will be able to work together as a unit and avoid tensions, misunderstandings, and conflicts.

Provide your UX design team members with constructive criticism rather than being negative because that will only put them down instead of helping.

Chapter 5
How To Build a Strong UX Culture

Building a great UX design culture starts with you, the UX manager. You need to set the standard on how things are done and ensure that everyone is abiding by these standards.

When you manage a creative team, culture is key. The right culture will help make your working environment inclusive and supportive. It's also essential in creating an environment where everyone contributes to the final product.

UX is not about building a pretty interface, it's all about making sure that design aligns with business goals while ensuring a smooth user experience.

You need to set goals and expectations and then work with the UX design team to meet those goals. You may need to re-communicate those goals as time goes on so that everyone understands what's expected of them, but this way you can address issues early on before they become problems.

When the culture of an organization is strong we mean that it's effective at producing the right results because the employees are engaged, communicating with each other easily and consistently producing value, and meeting customer needs.

Culture is how people behave because it's reinforced by the people around them. For example, if your UX design team members are constantly criticizing each other in public or sharing articles that don't contribute to work, you need to stop it immediately and address it with the person who has been exhibiting these behaviors. Only then can you build a user-focused culture.

There's a reason why companies have company values and mission statements. These are guidelines for everyone to follow and they're meant to be living documents that change over time. The whole point of having these guidelines is because you want all your employees to behave in a certain way which ultimately contributes to the growth of the business.

People get into UX design because they want to create great experiences. If there's no creative space where people can be innovative and express themselves then they will just go elsewhere. That's why you have to create a space for your employees to do great work by allowing them some creative freedom as well as providing the tools, resources, and support they need.

Ask yourself the following questions about the culture:

- Are people on the same page as far as what's expected from them?

- What kind of relationships and connections does everyone have with each other, internally and externally?

- Do we celebrate success together as a UX design team or do we only point out mistakes?

There are various questions to begin answering when establishing a UX culture.

While UX managers need to guide their team members, they can't be too harsh because this will break the morale of the UX design team. On the other hand, UX managers can't be too lenient because this will result in a lack of control over the UX design team and projects.

To successfully build a UX culture, you need to properly assess your team members. Go through each team member's strengths and weaknesses so that you know what kind of people you have on your side. This way, you will be able to assign tasks that are within everyone's reach and abilities.

An organization's culture directly affects its success on so many levels. It affects how employees feel about their work each day, and can have a huge impact on your company's ability to produce long-term success.

The best way to create this type of culture is by being transparent with the team, having fun when possible, listening when needed, hiring people who are passionate about what they do, and staying committed to your team.

- Be patient and consistent

Building a UX design culture doesn't happen overnight. It takes time to shape into successful changes that will be beneficial to the UX design team and organization. You might experiment with different things in the beginning, but you need to stick to them so they will become part of UX culture.

If you are consistent about what your UX design team needs to do for the company, then it won't take long for them to fully understand what they need to do. That means you will have cooperation instead of wasted time where everyone is unsure about the outcome.

- Be open to discussion

One thing that makes developing a UX design culture easier is allowing your team members to voice out their concerns and consider suggestions if it's beneficial for the company.

You need to be open for discussion among UX design team members so that if they see something you may not have noticed, they will still come and tell you. You can then work out a solution together rather than having them feel like nothing was done about it and it is their problem alone.

- Be flexible enough to change your decision or opinion when needed

Working with UX design team members can be unpredictable to an extent. You never know what will happen the next moment, so you need to accept that and make changes if necessary while still maintaining your leadership position.

- Regularly check in informally with your UX design team to ensure everything is going as planned

Always make it a point to check in with your team members to ensure that everything is going well for them. You can make it casual like asking about their weekend or how they're doing during lunchtime, but this way you will ensure that they are having fun at work and working hard.

You should also schedule progress reports with the UX design team so that you will know what they've been doing and can address any concerns they may have.

- Hold UX design team meetings to ensure everyone is working well together and no one is stepping on anyone's toes

You need to set up regular meetings with your UX design team so that everyone understands each other better and knows who is responsible for what tasks.

Regularly scheduled meetings will also allow you to address concerns with each member of the UX design team, especially if you noticed that someone is not working as hard or has been distracted.

It is important to understand your company's culture and what it stands for, because if you don't then you are risking the long-term success of your organization. A

Good culture will lead to better employee productivity and reduce turnover rates. If you want to create a great UX Culture in an organization, many things need to be considered.

The culture you should try to create should be based on the following: transparency, integrity, learning and development, fun-lovingness (inclusive of creativity), honesty, diversity (open-mindedness), and passion.

Here are some steps to help you create a great UX Culture for your organization:

Transparency

To have a good culture in an organization, transparency is needed. Transparency means that there is no hidden information from employees and vice versa.

You can do this by having open town hall meetings with the company, making public announcements about important issues, creating a blog about what's going on within the industry and how it relates to your business – basically making everything available to the public.

Showing all aspects of your business will help build trust amongst team members and customers/clients alike.

Integrity

Having high moral standards is very important for growing any type of relationship, whether it be personal or professional.

This stands true for building relationships within an organization.

Having integrity means that you are honest with your team, customers, and other stakeholders in the business. A simple way to accomplish this is by always following through on promises made towards others (customers or employees) and keep all agreements made.

Learning & Development

Companies need to continue learning new information every day which will help them build better products/services for their customers.

Because of this, companies must provide the necessary tools for their employees to grow professionally while they are working at the organization.

This can be done by holding public training classes quarterly using external speakers (from universities or trade organizations), setting up online courses which employees can take on their own time depending on what they need help with (while still reporting to the job they were hired for), and holding one on one meetings where employees can ask questions about what they are doing or other issues that may arise.

Create a culture of "fun" where we enjoy work

Having a culture that is fun, inclusive, and creative will help build better relationships within an organization.

This could be done by having team events like potlucks, company picnics in the summertime, lunch & learns from outside speakers, etc.

This type of environment encourages being creative when coming up with new concepts/ideas for product development. It also helps add diversity into your teams which will bring different perspectives to your projects which can lead to more well-rounded decisions in regards to design choices.

Not only that, but it is important to allow employees flexibility in their daily routine. Flexibility allows for more creativity and helps build trust between team members and the company they work for.

Honesty

It is very hard to build a culture of dishonesty because the truth always comes out eventually.

Strive to always be honest with your employees and your customers/clients so that when things do come out later on down the road it won't cause any unnecessary conflicts within the organization.

It can also give off a good impression for future job opportunities if anyone tries to apply at any of your business locations or partner companies with which you may have relationships (this happens quite often).

Diversity of Opinions and Backgrounds

For organizations to grow and succeed in any type of industry, they must have open-minded people running the business.

Having this quality means that your team will be more accepting of others who may have different ideas from their own. This will lead to a better environment for brainstorming and creativity which leads to innovative, outside-the-box thinking in regards to products/services you may provide. It also helps avoid any future conflicts between teams due to being narrow-minded.

People are happiest when they feel like part of a community—a group of people who share their values and interests—so chief among employee benefits today are opportunities for teamwork.

Social activities provide an excellent way to build teamwork skills while at the same time encouraging employees to get to know and respect each other better. They also just plain old have fun together, which is a key ingredient in employee retention.

The company should always strive towards improving its conditions by making sure the team has all the proper tools and equipment they need to do their job as efficiently as possible; both physically and mentally.

To effectively manage a team of UX professionals, it is important to be flexible and inclusive of all aspects.

This can be done by providing enjoyable work environments for their employees such as fun activities, social events, open-mindedness, and honesty.

You also need to make sure that your employees have everything they need to do their job and stimulate creativity (with comfortable furniture and TVs with streaming services like Netflix).

It is also necessary for companies to strive towards improvement by making sure the team has all the proper tools and equipment they need to do their job as efficiently as possible; both physically and mentally.

When you're in a leadership position, it is critical for you to know your limit because when something doesn't go as planned, people will look up to you for reassurance and say "It's OK. It won't happen again," or "Don't worry. I'll take care of it" when in fact you are just as concerned or worried about the issue at hand.

While it is a good thing that UX managers know how to calm people down and make them feel better, they need to learn how to react in a professional manner which means admitting what you don't know and saying that you will find out.

All managers should know how to keep their team members motivated and working hard without going overboard with criticism or rewards. Life is all about balance.

If a UX manager is too harsh on his/her UX design team members, they will be scared to make mistakes which in turn makes them look inept and a UX design leader who is too lenient on his/her UX design team members will be perceived as an ineffective leader.

As a UX manager, you need to know your limits and how far you can push your team before they lose interest or motivation regarding the task at hand.

Give Regular Feedback

UX design managers need to be especially mindful of their UXers, or else things can get out of hand or someone will quit. One important thing that UX managers should know is how to give good feedback because this impacts the team's morale and productivity.

Establish Clear Work Standards

UX managers need to establish clear work standards by laying out exactly what is expected of each UX design team member, whether it's establishing milestones with dates for key deliverables, or requiring that a UX design team member check in with you on an agreed-upon regular basis.

Ensure Everyone Focuses on Their Tasks

Besides building a culture, another thing that UX managers need to be mindful, or is keeping their team members focused on their tasks.

There are times when the UX design manager may have to refocus team members who are not fulfilling their responsibilities.

As a UX manager, you need to make sure that your team is focused on key deliverables which means giving them milestones with dates for each of these tasks and making sure nothing is getting in the way of their work.

A great way for management to demonstrate its commitment to UX is to provide resources that allow design teams and individual designers to be as creative as possible when working on projects, which may include funding for UX training or conferences or providing other types of resources designed specifically for UX professionals.

The company culture you create as a manager should support your team in every way, but creating a supportive environment is not always easy.

To grow a supportive and strong culture in a UX team, managers should:

- Seek the advice of team members.
- Actively promote their designers' successes and encour
- Make sure that team members know their contributions appreciated.
- Lead by example. Other departments may look to the UX it means to be a good leader, so make sure you have a p always doing your best.
- Show interest in their development and career goals, wh planning, mentoring, or just knowing where each person
- Help them understand the big picture of UX at your com within the product development cycle or the sequence c successful throughout an organization.
- Show up at design reviews and give useful feedback - n also opinions on presentation, process, and content.
- Listen carefully to their opinions and requests - they knc so whatever is discussed in these meetings should be p manager.
- Help guide them on any issues that come up such as cc situations with other departments or teams within your
- Celebrate design wins, both big and small.
- Organize team-building activities outside of work hours other better and, in turn, develop trust.
- Be transparent with your team regarding company plan:
- Give everyone a chance to ask questions or voice their c are being heard.

Another great way to promote the UX strength
within your company is to invite guest lecturers
from other departments or outside companies.

This will promote exposure to new ideas and keep employees from feeling as though they are trapped in a proverbial box that does not allow for creative thinking.

Every team member has different reasons for coming into work, and just because someone is excited about their job doesn't mean they're always productive. Some people are early birds while others are night owls; some have young families to attend to while others may be looking for ways to fill their free time. Understanding how your employees think can help you manage them better.

The most important thing to remember is that a UX team's culture is only as strong as its members. A manager should be looking for ways to help employees grow, not just meeting their expectations or fulfilling their needs for the day. There will always be days when people feel under-appreciated and unhappy, but managers can help bolster the team's morale by finding ways to bring out the best in each member.

In summary, the culture of your UX team sets the tone of your UX efforts, so taking the time to set up a team culture filled with respect and motivation for advocating for users will result in maximum productivity.

Culture is also one of the most difficult things to change in a team, but it's an area where UX managers can make a huge impact.

Chapter 6
How to Measure the ROI of Your UX

ROI or return on investment is one of the most commonly-used terms in business, but it can be hard to know what exactly it means for UX.

In the perfect world, a UX manager has unlimited resources and can invest in all areas where design and usability improvement can positively impact business metrics. But this isn't a perfect world, so it's important to know how to determine which UX activities provide the best return on investment for your company.

You can measure the ROI of your UX activities by looking at the costs associated with the design and research process and dividing that number by the revenue that the changes generate or the cost savings they create by preventing undesirable outcomes like customer churn or bounce rates, user errors or frustration, or helpdesk service tickets. It's hard to measure things like goodwill or brand value, but it's impossible not to invest in these areas when you accurately understand the payoff to the bottom line.

Consider some of these facts about the return on investment of UX:

- AirBnB's founder, Joe Gebbia mainly attributes UX desi product with their incredible growth and their current $1
- Wal-Mart's online division saw a traffic increase of more redesigned the UX of their website
- Hubspot saw a 300% improvement in their website's co project improved their usability and design

If you're anything like me, you sometimes find yourself trying to justifying to someone spending additional resources improving designs or advocating for users even though the improvements aren't immediately noticeable on the company's income statement.

You want to know what are the key areas that if you invest wisely, could yield huge improvements for the users and improve your company's bottom line at the same time.

The first step: Get curious about your users. Start with qualitative feedback and customer interactions- what are the most common questions or problems your customers are having? What can you learn from those insights, and how can your designs evolve to better meet user needs?

Open-ended surveys and interviews provide an opportunity for deeper research and allow UX managers to retain more control over the data they are collecting.

Since UX professionals are experts at design research, getting curious about your company's data is one of the best ways to demonstrate ROI for UX work. Asking questions, then using that information to affect change will prove the usefulness of investing in user experience daily.

The second step: Look at the quantitative data - is there more traffic or conversions? More blog comments, email subscriptions, social shares, fewer helpdesk tickets?

See what areas have grown since you've been doing UX work. If the assumptions in your design improvements are correct, then in a perfect world all of these numbers should have increased as well.

Of course, it's also important to assign a value to each of these metrics. Many companies have very specific ways of assigning value to "cost-per-customer-acquisition" and sometimes are willing to spend an incredible amount to retain an existing or attract a new customer.

Also, look at more complicated metrics like customer satisfaction and churn - if they've increased, was it before or after you've implemented UX research and design updates?

The third and final step: Compare baseline data with a time series. This is a great way to see the direct effects of your UX work overtime, and this adjusted view will help you have a more nuanced understanding of how design affects business metrics.

The important with baseline metrics is to collect as much data as possible before beginning work on your UX projects, then to compare the same metrics post-UX work using the same tools.

The most difficult part about all of these steps is getting access to users and user data as well as company metrics and data about conversions and usability improvement impacts on business goals.

Remember, correlation doesn't always equal causation - which means that even though something happened before another change, it doesn't mean that one thing caused the other. We need to be careful in our research to determine causation.

One easy way to collect user feedback is by using remote methods, such as surveys or online polls. This option works well when you are looking to capture the UX team's overall progress or contributions within a certain timeframe. It can also be used when you don't have the resources in place to collect data directly from customers in real-time, which happens in some industries more than others.

Look at your UX process itself by measuring how quickly and efficiently your team is completing their tasks. This option offers a great way to measure UX success when you're looking at how well the team works as a whole and their understanding of the design process.

More specifically, if you are measuring customer acquisition or retention through UX processes, then you will find that every effective touchpoint with a customer leads to increased revenue and allows your company to justify your existence as a business.

The best way to measure is to consider what your organization does well as a whole. Look at how effective each UX team member is in their role and how well they interact with the rest of the company. You can then benchmark these factors against other UX teams to determine which activities led to your success.

If you aren't sure which success metrics are right for your company, start by identifying what customers value and what they are trying to accomplish when using a product or service.

This means identifying where your customers might drop off during their user journey, or where they are not experiencing the best possible outcome. You can then measure success by looking at how these metrics have changed after implementing UX research and design updates.

You'll notice a shift in numbers - maybe it's not as big as you think, but the shift will show how much better-informed design decisions are after getting curious about user behavior, conducting research, and analyzing the ROI of your UX.

Chapter 7
How to Manage UX Design Without Micromanaging

As a UX manager, it's important to strike a balance between autonomy and control when working with your team.

You need to know when to be flexible and when to be ridged and toe the line. Choose your battles wisely and you will gain more trust and respect from your team.

Remember that UX designers are part of a larger design process and design should always be iterative. You should strive to get the best product possible while delivering it within a given time frame. There will never be a perfect solution, so keep improving your designs based on new requirements and inputs from stakeholders and members of your team.

If you are concerned about UX designers pulling their weight, then make sure you are giving them the proper tools, techniques, and guidance they need to be successful. Essentially, managers can help maximize productivity by ensuring that everyone on the team has everything she needs to get her job done right.

By setting clear goals and providing direction in the early stages of any project, you'll avoid unnecessary reworks that can often be attributed to poor communication.

There is a fine line between micromanaging your team and letting them free to do their best work. Ideally, you want to create a balance between responsibility and accountability where you give them the freedom and position and tools to perform, then hold them accountable to show you that they are worth the price you're paying for their services and they are benefitting the UX team.

But this doesn't mean that you need to treat every single UX designer on your team the same. You should take into consideration the level of experience of the UX worker, as well as the difficulty of the project, your available resources, and so on. Some of your employees might be most valuable when they are allowed to work autonomously and solve problems on their own.

By offering a high degree of autonomy to some members of your team while taking a more hands-on approach with others, you can allow your whole team to work at their full potential while still providing the oversight that you need as a UX manager to meet your goals.

The key is to differentiate between times that require hands-on direction and those that are better suited to autonomy, then tailor your approach accordingly.

For example, if you are working on a project that has strict deadlines, or is a high profile project - or if your UX team itself is understaffed or has several new members- then it's often best to take a proactive role, especially in the early stages of the design process.

You can also employ different styles of management depending on how well an individual responds to autonomy versus direction. For example, some designers work best when they are given a clear goal and then left to complete tasks on their own. Others would benefit from step-by-step instructions throughout the entire process and constant feedback and communication.

Use different leadership styles and adjust your strategy based on the requirements of the specific tasks at hand.

By understanding when your team members work best, and selecting an appropriate approach for each designer or UX professional, you can better ensure everyone's success.

Solving this issue without stepping on any toes can be difficult, even for experienced managers.

The bottom line is this, your employees want to do a good job and take pride in their work. Show them that you're willing to support them by offering guidance and feedback whenever it's needed, but you trust them to do good work on their own. Trust but verify and hold everyone accountable.

This style of "Management by walking around" shows your team that you're not too good to get involved in the day-to-day work that makes everything possible.

But it's important to remember that there's a time and place for everything and in addition to keeping an eye on employees via check-ins and one-on-one sessions, you should also take the time to give your team freedom to work alone or with each other without the boss always watching.

While I was at MIT, I heard something incredible about worker satisfaction. They said that one of the biggest predictors of if an organization's employees are happy in their work or not had nothing to do with what most people would think. It's not about how much money you make, or how cool your office is, no...

What they found was that the biggest predictor of employee satisfaction was autonomy and control over delivering valuable work. In other words, how much input and control employees were given over what they did, and how positive they felt about their ability to be useful and valuable to others was the biggest predictor of their satisfaction with their careers.

Okay, maybe that's a bit grandiose to always let your UX team run wild... But the point is, give them some space to manage themselves, but make sure they are aware of your goals and expectations. It doesn't matter if you're an enterprise-level UX manager or someone running a small design team, the idea is to provide autonomy and set your expectations high.

With good UX leadership like this, your team can work efficiently without making mistakes that you might have made if you were in their shoes.

Of course, when deadlines or budgets are tight and timelines are short, the entire process will likely need more oversight and management than usual.

In summary, give your team autonomy and responsibility whenever possible. If you hired the right people, their performance will increase rather than decrease with more freedom. However, if the project is particularly demanding or high profile, go ahead and manage your team more closely. They'll be glad that you helped them deliver a quality product on time.

Freedom married with accountability helps you meet your goals while allowing employees to take pride in the work that they do every day.

Chapter 8
How to Inspire Great Designs and Keep Team Morale High

Your UX team needs to be happy and engaged to do their best work and keep morale high. Team morale is important for the success of any organization, but it becomes especially critical when it comes to UX teams.

Your UX team members are often responsible for working on difficult and highly visible projects that can take months or even years to complete from start to finish.

Even UX designers who are highly experienced can quickly become disillusioned if they feel that their work isn't valued or that their ideas aren't being heard by the rest of your organization.

I can say that almost every UX project I've worked on has encountered setbacks and challenges at some point during the project. Sometimes I've even had team members abandon the project or asked to be moved onto another project that's easier or didn't present as many challenges.

There are times when it's best to move onto another project you're better suited for, but there's also something to be said for gritting your teeth and deciding you're not going to quit until you've solved the problem at hand.

As the UX manager, you don't have the luxury of quitting and you need to set an example for your team. So how do you foster the kind of morale that will convince UX designers to stick with a project even when it seems like the going is tough?

Focus on what's working – No matter how difficult a project might be, find something positive about it and focus on that. It could be anything from the usefulness of a certain feature or something that works well technically or a new tool that could help the team's UX efforts. When things get difficult, remind yourself and your team of the end goal and keep everyone's eyes on the prize.

Sometimes the journey seems like 1,000 miles and when you encounter difficulties you need to remind everyone to keep going and not give up. You will need to do everything in your power to keep their spirits high throughout the process.

Remind everyone why they're there –

As a UX manager, you need to make sure your UX designers understand how what they do benefits the company by increasing customer loyalty, benefits the users by improving their lives in some way, and serves to benefit everyone else in the organization by improving the level of value that they can provide to their customers.

In some cases, this might require a little bit of work on your part because you'll need to explain why their role is important within the company's business model. But this shouldn't be difficult to grasp and once people understand what they're working towards, morale should improve and your team will become more productive.

Promote work-life balance among employees –

Having a healthy work-life balance is important for any UX manager because it ensures that UX designers are happy both at home and at work. While there will usually be times when they need to put in extra effort, you should encourage them to take regular breaks, go on vacation when needed and make sure you're open to considering flexible working arrangements such as working from home, part-time hours, or other options depending on your company's culture and the type of work UX designers do.

Emphasize accountability –

As a UX manager, it's important to be honest and straightforward with your team members and let them know exactly how they're doing and what they need to do to improve.

Invest in trust-building –

The UX manager needs to foster a culture of trust within their organization, which can be achieved by sharing information and giving people the freedom to make decisions without having to check every decision with you first. You should encourage your team members to come up with their strategies and give them the space they need to do things in their way while still keeping you informed along the way.

UX design is often a collaborative effort and it's important to create an environment where everyone can contribute their ideas with confidence that they will be heard and acknowledged by the rest of the team, no matter how junior or senior someone might be. Consensus building is crucial for success and your UX designers need to feel

Go beyond "My door is always open" -

"My door is always open" doesn't mean anything to anyone. UX managers need to let their team members know that meetings, feedback, and other communication won't be limited to scheduled times or certain days of the week. Sticking by that statement only makes sense if you go beyond it and are available for your team whenever they want to meet or need help with something.

Run your design process as a democracy-

As UX manager, you need to ensure that the entire company is on board regarding UX design and that everyone understands what UX designers are doing. This includes management so they don't step in at the wrong times, customers who will be using any software developed

Give teammates a chance to interact outside the office–

A great way to strengthen relationships between UX design team members is to encourage them to socialize outside the office. Allowing your team members to have lunch together, go out for a drink after work, or participate in various sports will help them get along with each other and develop trust. In some companies, UX managers even organize company events such as barbeques, team lunches, and dinners.

Support employee-led initiatives -

UX design is a team sport and if your team members want to develop or pursue something that will benefit the company as a whole, then you need to support them and help them get it done. This could be anything from setting up workshops so they can share knowledge, forming teams for specific projects, or allowing people to spend time working on their own "side projects" when they don't have anything else in the pipeline.

You will be working with people who are passionate about UX design and this means that you should expect them to come up with ideas for new initiatives or projects that could help your company improve its customer experience. Encourage your team members to submit proposals for new projects and initiatives and if you see one that will benefit the company as a whole, then give it your full support.

As a UX manager, you shouldn't be worried about employees going behind your back to get things done because this often happens when people feel like they aren't being listened to or heard by their managers. To avoid this, you need to create an environment where all your employees feel comfortable coming to you with their ideas and concerns.

UX work is all about improving the customer experience which means that it should be driven by everyone in the company, not just UX designers. You can take this one step further by fostering a culture of innovation among your team members so that everyone is constantly coming up with new ideas and ways of improving the user experience, not just UX designers.

Employees should feel like they are part of a team that has an important goal, which is to improve customer satisfaction by providing great UX design services or products that meet people's needs. When this happens, it creates an environment where your

Don't ignore the power of small gestures-

As a UX manager, you should never underestimate the power of simple things like remembering your team members' birthdays or congratulating them on their wedding or children's accomplishments. Little gestures can go a long way in making people feel appreciated and loved so don't be afraid to give out hugs or thank people when they do something good for the company.

Celebrate the achievement of milestones –

If your team is working on something that's broken down into smaller deliverables, celebrate each one as you go along. Celebrating milestones doesn't necessarily mean throwing a big party or kudos all around. It can take any form- whether it be an email to the entire team acknowledging their efforts, or a nice email to the UX designer who contributed most to the milestone, or even a small gift. In my experience, I've seen morale skyrocket when people realize that they're making progress towards an objective and also being acknowledged for their efforts and contributions to the team.

Another way of motivating your worker is to place them in a good work environment. It is extremely important that your workplace design is comfortable and welcoming so employees can be comfortable working together. Make sure they have adequate supplies needed to produce the best results for their projects.

An essential part of motivating employees is setting goals with them. You will want to set goals with each employee individually as well as with the team as a whole. It is important to meet with employees at least six weeks before their goal deadline, so you can discuss the approach they plan to take and how it meshes with the company's overall goals.

Smart managers know that it is important to both cultivate and bring out the best in UX designers. In some aspects, you need to form a connection with them. You need to provide them with the resources that they need for them to do their job well, teach them or give them books on design, motivate them by setting a good example, and making sure you respect each of their opinions.

As a UX team leader, you cannot simply throw tasks at your UX team without giving any direction or instruction on how they should go about doing those tasks. That is why when you are facing problems with your UX team, it is necessary to be able to understand what the problem might be. You need to remember that each member of your design team comes with different sets of strengths and weaknesses.

Good UX managers always try to bring out the best in their UX team members. They remember to celebrate big accomplishments, give constant feedback on how they can improve, and motivate them through small gestures that bring personal recognition.

Motivating your UX workers is essential because it will help you produce good results for your company. It also increases the morale of employees so they are more motivated to work hard.

By understanding the needs and wants of each member of your design team, you will be able to work with them effectively and efficiently. This will help you avoid problems and conflicts that can arise when you don't know how your employees think or what they want.

Motivating your team by creating an environment to allow your UX designers to do what they love is something that managers should consider. Motivating employees by giving them more freedom and flexibility for their work can help push them towards excellence. For example, creating a space where they feel good and comfortable such as an office with the perfect temperature and lighting will affect how your designs will turn out because it gives your UX designer inspiration for his or her work.

While you are motivating your UX team, it is also necessary for you to keep things interesting by giving them challenges that can improve their skills. Managers should approach these challenges carefully though as it needs creativity and observation so that the UX designer may not feel overwhelmed with his/her task at hand. If possible, use resources within your reach such as books or other resources online which includes templates and information about wire-framing so that UX Designers don't have to spend too much time

Lead the team by ensuring you design a UX Team Structure that will work for you and your company. Assigning tasks based on strengths, weaknesses, and interests of individuals in the UX design team. The importance of understanding how each person's role is important to the success of the team as a whole. Find ways to help maintain creativity among designers (i.e., providing time outside work or giving them constructive criticism) Also, keeping in mind the team's overall morale and motivation when assigning tasks.

Understand your UX team's dynamics is the key to manage different personalities within a team. Understanding how your team members will work best with each other (i.e., working independently or in small groups) and establishing ground rules for interaction between UX designers (i.e., no interruptions while someone is focused on completing something) is important. Having regular meetings to discuss design issues and concerns. Building trust among team members through better communications via constructive feedback, open lines of communication, etc.

Once you have determined what types of tasks each member of the UX design team should specialize in, create an environment that motivates them so they feel good about coming to work every day.

Understanding how everyone works together will enable you to assign tasks so that your UX design team can keep the work on track without too many distractions.

It's your responsibility to show team members that their work is valued and that you're committed to seeing their projects through no matter how difficult things seem at times.

The bottom line is this: If team morale stays high, then your chances of success go up dramatically.

Build a positive work culture: Remind yourself and your team why you're passionate about what you do by aligning your UX efforts with business goals.

Focus on the end goal: Keep your eye on the prize- a better user experience for everyone involved.

Celebrate small milestones: A simple thank you goes a long way to show team members that their work is being valued and appreciated.

Build a positive work culture, focus on the end goal, celebrate small milestones, and have fun.

All of these things can be used to keep morale high and keep your UX team productive and engaged.

Chapter 9
Managing Remote UX Teams in a Post-COVID World

Since the start of the COVID-19 global pandemic, and subsequent social distancing measures, technology work is almost completely gone remote. UX design is now remote, and if the UX design team is remote, then managers will need to develop different management strategies that can help them stay on track while working on distributed teams.

How do you motivate people if they're not in the same room as you?

Two of the most talented UX designers I've ever met live thousands of miles from me and I've never actually been in the same room as them physically. Olivia lives in Ukraine and Rebecca lives in the Philippines.

Neither of them has ever been to the US, either. Their work is fantastic and I can review it over Zoom video meetings regularly

Creating successful designs remotely can come with its own unique set of opportunities and challenges. No longer do we need to be physically close to UX team members to accomplish great work.

But we do need to know how to focus and align the UX team to create a cohesive and unified user experience.

When it comes to managing remote teams, many unique challenges come with the territory. For example, because you can't see your team every day in person, it may be difficult to maintain a sense of camaraderie or know how they're feeling about projects.

It is up to the UX manager to create a highly engaging environment where team members feel engaged and comfortable speaking their minds and being honest about how they feel.

For UX managers, it is important to create a sense of trust within the team that enables members to feel comfortable giving each other critical feedback.

When people hold back on giving feedback, they are usually not being disagreeable but are being respectful by withholding the bluntest observations until trust is stronger.

Because they don't trust you completely, they don't feel like they can be honest with how they feel about you. Be suspicious if people start to act guarded or quiet around you, this may show that they don't yet trust you to the point that they feel like they can openly and freely share how they feel with you.

Open communication helps UX managers better understand their team members so that they can help to establish trust. UX team members must be comfortable with each other to have frank conversations about concerns they have on either side.

It is also important to maintain regular contact with your team members for them to feel included and part of the team, not just a remote worker out of sight. UX managers should implement different types of communication tools that will help the whole team stay connected regularly where they can share ideas.

Messaging services like Slack and Teams help teams communicate, and video conferencing tools like Zoom give us a first-person view.

As a UX Manager, it's difficult to guarantee that remote teams feel included and have a sense of belonging, but the most essential thing is to establish an atmosphere where workers feel comfortable expressing their views and being honest about how they're feeling.

Because you can't see your remote team every day in person, managing them presents its own set of difficulties.

The key for building UX Culture for a remote team is to remember that your team is made up of individuals, each one unique with its strengths and weaknesses.

How you communicate with one person may not be the best way to communicate with another, so it's important to tailor your approach for each individual.

Another tip for building a feel-good remote environment is to have chats about what people are working on or talking about. You can do this through daily 'standup meetings' where everyone updates everyone else on what they've been working on.

Whether it be daily or less often, ensure to integrate video chats at least once a week - it can help build trust among colleagues if they know each other's voices and faces well enough.

Make sure you set shared goals for all members to work toward. This keeps everyone working in the same direction, rather than side by side with no particular destination in mind.

Remote management is a new learning curve for many managers.

The benefits of remote management are that you can hire more people in areas where there is a lack of talent, while the challenge is making sure that employees feel valued and included in the company culture.

With that being said, here are three tips on how to include remote teams in your UX workflow:

1. Update employees often about the company's progress

Keep them involved in what's going on behind the scenes. This will make them feel like they're an integral part of the team even though they may be miles away.

2. Hold weekly all-hands UX team meetings

Where everyone updates each other on their projects/goals/milestones, even if it's just a short meeting via video chat or Google Hangouts. These weekly updates are effective because then everyone knows what everyone else is working on at all times. Some apps to get started with are Skype, Google Hangouts, etc...

3. Encourage face-to-face interaction and collaboration

A lot of companies have moved towards remote work due to world events or the lack of talent in certain geographical areas, but it's up to the UX manager to create an environment that encourages workers from different areas to share their perspectives freely without fear of rejection or exclusion.

The goal is to help managers create an environment that prevents remote teams from feeling excluded. This goal is achieved by making the critical effort of communicating with them often, finding out what they're working on and what they need to accomplish their goals. This will create a sense of community among team members in addition to creating a culture in which honesty can thrive.

Your remote employees are your greatest asset in terms of talent, but that doesn't mean they're any less important than the people who work in the office every day. Every team member is crucial to UX success, and it's up to you as a manager to make sure remote workers are included in all aspects of your culture.

it's difficult to guarantee that remote teams feel included and have a sense of belonging but building an atmosphere of trust and honest communication is a great first step.

The key to including remote teams in your culture and workflow is to communicate often, aim for regular meetings where everyone updates each other on their projects, and also encourage face-to-face interaction by encouraging your team members to meet up in real life at least once every couple months. This will not only strengthen personal relationships but also help build a culture of trust and honesty.

Don't worry, you can survive as a remote UX Manager. It's easy if you remember to follow these steps:

1) Communicate often and aim for weekly meetings with all team members

2) Encourage face-to-face interaction and collaboration by getting your teams together at least once every couple of months

3) Create an environment that prevents remote workers from feeling excluded by building a culture of trust and honesty.

It's difficult to guarantee that remote teams are always engaged, but if you follow these three guidelines, you'll likely be able to successfully lead your UX team remotely.

Chapter 10
Becoming a UX Leader and Not Just a Manager

Ultimately, your goal as a UX Manager is to rise to the level of a UX Leader. Leadership is different than management. Anyone can be a manager, but only a few can be leaders.

One of the biggest distinctions between managers and leaders is that people willing want to follow leaders, but will only obey managers when it is required by their jobs. Leaders inspire people to work hard and do amazing things, while managers tell people what to do and have a hard time getting them to follow orders without question or debate.

A great leader is someone who can pass their vision on effectively through words, visual presentations, and even body language. They understand that leadership is not about commanding or forcing people to do something they don't want to do, but rather about inspiring and influencing your team into following your lead because they want to do it.

You need to create a compelling vision and bring it into reality. You need to explain your role as UX professionals, that you advocate and support every user, especially the ones who are having difficulty using your product or service. You need to explain to your team how what you're doing is special and makes a real difference in people's lives every day. By creating this connection, you can bring out the best in people and inspire them to create great experiences.

This is the key difference between leadership and management; anyone can be appointed as a manager, but only those who can inspire loyalty and action can be leaders.

Another distinction between managers and leaders is that leaders create an emotional connection to what they're doing and between team members. They have a passion for what they do and can express that passion through their messaging, tone of voice, body language, and more. Their passion for UX is contagious and they cause everyone to produce better work.

Leadership is one of the most difficult things to develop in a team member because it's not something that can be forced or predicted. You can only inspire others with your leadership instead of trying to make people follow you.

To become a great UX leader, focus on the following:

1) Focus on building emotional connections between team members. Passion is contagious.

2) Don't try to force anyone to do something they don't want to do. Influencing their behavior through inspiration is better than forcing them into action.

3) Be patient! It takes time for people's natural talents to develop into leaders.

4) Be open and honest with everyone on your team and encourage them to be the same with you.

5) don't micromanage, but rather give people the freedom to try their ideas without feeling too much pressure.

6) Help others to grow and improve as leaders whenever possible.

7) Create an atmosphere of trust and honesty where everyone feels comfortable being honest with each other about what's working and what isn't.

UX leadership begins with emotional connections between team members, so don't try to force anyone into doing something they don't want to do. Inspire them instead of forcing their hand by encouraging honest communication and building a culture of trust and honesty.

Inspire others to follow your lead, because they want to follow, instead of commanding them or forcing them. As a UX Manager, your job is to inspire and lead a group of talented and diverse professionals.

All great leaders are not only knowledgeable of their craft, but they are also balanced, fair, and open-minded. They lead with confidence, but flexibility with the ultimate goal of serving everyone around them.

They are very firm and fixed on the end goal of improving the user experience, but flexible in their approach, overcoming any challenges or obstacles. UX Leaders never give up and always go the extra mile to help others achieve success. They understand that everyone needs some guidance along the way to grow, so they are ready to provide advice when necessary.

UX Leadership is about being confident in your approach without being too rigid. That's the very essence of UX Leadership.

To improve as a leader, it's also important to read books and watch YouTube lectures that have been put out by other great UX leaders. These are just a few examples to get you started:

* The 21 Irrefutable Laws of Leadership, by John Maxwell

* The 48 Laws of Power, by Robert Greene

* The 5 Dysfunctions of a Team, by Patrick Lencioni

It's important to read books from people who have been successful as leaders so you can learn from their successes and mistakes. As always though, remember not to simply imitate what they've done because it won't work for you.

Instead of imitating their actions, try to understand the common leadership principles that all these leaders use and apply them to your leadership style.

You can also read biographies of great leaders and draw inspiration from their success stories.

There are many online resources for UX management methods, but the most important thing you should take away from this article is that leadership begins

Many people have been confused with leadership and management because these terms seem to be interchangeable. While being a good manager will help develop strong leadership skills, you cannot expect everyone to become a leader just by managing them. People chose to follow inspiring leaders, but anyone can be a manager.

Great leaders are not always naturals who can lead groups of people with ease. To become a great leader one must have the ability to communicate effectively with their peers while inspiring them along the way.

Great leaders seek out feedback, new ideas, and the opinions of others so they can continue to adapt and grow. Great leaders understand that even if you're the boss, you're still human.

Good leaders are open to ideas and new ways of thinking, even if they ultimately disagree with a proposed approach. They also give credit where it's due and praise their team members for a job well done.

The best leaders are not afraid to ask for help, and they know that asking questions is what makes them better at their job.

And most importantly, great leaders know that success is not an end goal – it's a daily commitment to achieving a common goal. If you're lucky, you'll work for a great leader at some point in your career because they are inspiring to be around and can cause everyone around them to grow and accomplish more.

Being a successful UX manager is about building trust with your team members so that they can do their best work without feeling micromanaged.

Lead with confidence but stay open-minded - good leaders must be willing to accept new ideas and think on their feet. Get feedback from your team members - great leaders know that working in isolation will never produce the best work.

Understand that even though you're in charge, you are still human and everyone makes mistakes. When you make a mistake, admit it and learn from the mistake so you can grow as a manager. Nobody likes or trusts a leader who can't admit they were wrong at times.

As a leader, it's essential to ask for help when you need it- all successful leaders have made this a priority.

And lastly, you shouldn't make it your goal to be the "Cool boss" or have your main goal to be liked by your UX team... your main goal should be advocating for the user and providing the best user experience possible.

Although being liked by your team should not be your main goal, I've found that if you treat everyone kindly and respectfully, while maintaining high UX design and research standards, I think you'll be surprised by how many people grow to not only like you but respect and admire what you're doing for the team. You're able to get things done and keep everything on track will win you the supporters who matter.

You also eventually want every member of your UX team to develop into a leader in their own right because great leadership is the key to having a successful organization.

However, it takes time for people to become leaders, even if they have the necessary skills. Don't get discouraged if you don't see results right away, it takes time for people to grow and learn.

Leadership is a huge responsibility and shouldn't be taken lightly. You have the lives of designers and researchers in your hands and if you don't do a good job you could cause untold stress and hardship for your team members. You need to make sure you're always looking out for the team and doing what is best for them.

Remember great leaders don't know it all or have all the answers, but they do care about and have compassion for the members of their team. They watch out for their team and help them nurture their career to become better leaders themselves.

In the end, leadership is about making sure that the people you work with are happy and successful. In many ways, your UX team's ultimate experience is a direct result of how well you lead them...and let's face it – everyone wants to work for a great leader!

Conclusion

The highest goal is to rise from being a UX Manager to becoming a true UX Leader.

There is a key difference. Any company can appoint someone as a manager, but only a leader will inspire others to want to follow them and create great work.

You don't need to be loud or an extrovert to be a leader, but you do need to have a strong vision and be able to communicate that vision with your UX team.

UX leaders can help others within their organization by being a trusted source of assistance, who is knowledgeable in UX and can translate it when communicating with non-UX professionals.

The challenges of leading UX teams won't ever really go away; they'll just change because there will be different people involved. It's also important to remember that not everyone will like you, but if they respect you, then that's all that is required to create great experiences for the users. After all, it's not about you or your UX team, it's all about the user and their experience.

For you to excel as a UX Manager, you must have strong leadership qualities as well as an understanding of the business goals and key performance indicators of the company or organization. Remember that being successful at your job means balancing both design priorities with business goals so make sure you're doing what needs to be done to maximize profitability while delivering the best user experience.

You should always lead by example when dealing with team members, clients, stakeholders—everyone.

User Research focuses on understanding user expectations, needs, and behaviors through methodical and investigative approaches. Insights are then used to ensure that all the product design decisions are made to benefit the user.

Any UX designer can create a fresh design, but only a skilled designer knows how to craft a cohesive set of designs that work together to deliver an excellent user experience. Having a stunning idea or design is most probably going to be useless if the product is inconvenient to use or isn't integrated into a larger experience that delivers value for users.

A total of 7 factors influence a user's experience of your product or service.

Let us take a look at each factor in turn and what it means for the overall user experience:

1. USEFUL: If a product is not useful to someone, why would you want to bring it to the market? If it has no purpose, it is highly unlikely to be able to compete for attention alongside a market full of purposeful and useful products. This is a major factor that affects the customers' view of the product. As practitioners, we cannot be content with painting within the lines drawn by managers.

We must have the courage and creativity to ask whether our products and systems are useful, to be able to apply our knowledge of craft and medium to define innovative solutions that are more useful. It is worth noting that "useful" is in the eye of the beholder and things can be deemed "useful" if they deliver non-practical benefits.

The chances of a useful feature, website, or even an app to succeed among users are highly likely when compared to something unnecessary. Good designers often plan how they can make their work seem useful to users, that ought to be the aim anyways. An organization should launch the product to meet customer needs.

People are more obsessed to purchase a brand or company product that yields better results, quickly and effectively. When you make products that are not useful for the customer, they might get a bad impression on it. This might even let them doubt purchasing other goods from the company in the long run. So, make sure that you are delivering the products that are useful for the customers in a vast manner.

2.   USABLE: Usability is concerned with enabling users to effectively and efficiently achieve their end objective with a product, service, or website. The products or services that are offered by your company should be ready to use. In addition, you must support the users to achieve their goals effectively. So, it is deemed necessary to consider the usability feature as critical and develop the products.

The first generation of the products or services is more likely to contain less usability, that just be rectified in the second generation, and it should be continued like that to an advanced level.

Sometimes you see products succeed even if they are not usable, but especially with the growing number of well-designed products, this is less and less likely. Let us say you have added a useful feature to your website or app, but if it is not usable, it will ruin the whole user experience.

Think of it as using fancy icons minus the accompanying labels. You can use tooltips, but instead of putting the information right away, you are only adding to the overall user input time. Designers of the product or service must make sure that all the features and options added are easily usable. It is never a good idea to give your users a more-or-less half-baked design.

3.   FINDABLE: What good are astounding designs and a healthy amount of useful information and features if the users cannot find them? A findable user experience refers to the idea that the product must be easy to find
and in the instance, of digital and information products; the content within them must be easy to find too. If you cannot find a product, you are not going to buy it and this is true for all potential users of that product. Hence, it is crucial to present the necessary information to the right users and at the right moment as well.

Letting your users waste their time figuring out what a button or an element is supposed to do, or where they should go to do something is not very effective. The more steps it takes to do something, the more your users are going to feel pestered. This is not good for the image of the product, service or website. We must strive to design navigable websites and locatable objects, so users can find what they need and organizations must promote their product or service to publish theirs amid society. Only then people would come to know about your business and reach you to fulfill their needs. The findability feature is very essential for businesses. Findability adds a vital impact to the user experience of many products.

4.   CREDIBLE: Trust is an important factor and should never be taken for granted. Credibility directly translates to how trustworthy the information on your website or app is. Without trust, customers will not buy any product or service from you or your company.

Randall Terry said; "Fool me once, shame on you. Fool me twice, shame on me." Users of today are not going to give you a second chance to fool them. They are plenty of options in nearly every field for them to choose a credible product provider. Credibility relates to the ability of the user to trust in the product that you have provided.

Not just that it does the job that it is supposed to do but that it will last for a reasonable amount of time, also that the information provided with it is accurate and fit-for-purpose.

It is nearly impossible to deliver a successful user experience if the users think the product creator has bad intentions. The trust of the customers in your product or service is termed as the credible factor of user experience. As customers are spending their time as well as money in your company, you should never fail to deliver your quality service. Also, implement various business strategies such as adding testimonials, portfolios, or partner references to improve the credibility of your business. The trust that you build for your brand among people goes a long way in the success of your product, service, or website.

5.   DESIRABLE:
So you have created something credible, useful, and usable,

but have you made sure it is desirable by the users? Being desirable means that your product, service, or website is used and appreciated by someone who found it extremely well made. The desirable factor is nothing but reaching a high purchase of your product or service in the target market. The most-welcomed products have a more desirable feature for their brand, design, usage, and cost.

The improvement of desirable factors will help you to get more customers to be satisfied with your product, thereby enhancing your business. Hence, a company should put much effort to aid improvement to the value of your brand. The desirable factor is measured when you have a comeback of satisfied customers which plays a vital role in enhancing your business.

What if users found out something better than the best you have to offer? Desirability is converted in design through elements like branding, imaging, company lifestyle, identity, aesthetics, and emotional designs. The more desirable a product—the more likely it is that the user who has it will brag about it and create the desire in other users as well. It is recommended to put efforts into creating a well-planned design to help expand its reach.

Customer satisfaction is key to bring desirable as users are always on the lookout for a good user experience. A good user experience leaves a positive impression of your product, service, or website on its users. It is therefore essential to increase your brand value which could result in a better user experience.

"Want your users to fall in love with your designs? Fall in love with your users." - Dana Chassell.

6. ACCESSIBLE: Sadly, accessibility often gets lost in the mix when creating user experiences. Accessibility is about providing an experience that can be accessed by users of a full range of abilities- this includes those who are disabled in some respect
such ad hearing loss, impaired vision, motion-impaired or learning impaired. Accessibility is one of the essential factors of user experience which denotes the introduction of a product or service and making the same access to all kinds of people.

For instance, physically challenged people should benefit from your business. The products made should not be created for a certain community as it can result in deteriorating the value of your brand. It is important to create a good strategic plan while deciding to start a business which would help develop accessible products for society.

Accessibility features may include; screen readers, magnifiers, color filters, high contrast text, captions, speech recognition. It is up to the designers to implement some if not all accessibility features in their design. Design for accessibility is often seen by companies as a waste of money because the impression is that people with disabilities make up a small segment of the population, whereas that is not true. It is also worth remembering that when you design for accessibility, you will often find that you create products that are easier for everyone to use and not just those with disabilities. Do not neglect accessibility in the user experience.

7. VALUABLE: Everything is designed, few things are designed well. After considering all the above factors, we must not forget about the delivered value. A good user experience translates to a higher value of the design.

Value refers to being able to provide a user experience that is enriching to the lives of your consumers. Whenever you deliver a product or service, ensure that it brings the best results which add value to your brand. The product must deliver value. The lack of value on either side may spoil your business reputation. It must deliver value to the business which creates it and to the user who buys or uses it. Without value, likely any initial success of a product will eventually be undermined. You should never build a product that does not create value.

The final design must be of excellent quality to enhance its value. A design's worth can be measured by the cost of problems it solves. Nothing is more effective than an inexpensive design solving an expensive design problem. Design your business in such a way that it boosts up your reputation rather than lowering it. In addition to this, you can improve the user experience or value factor by providing chances for customers to say their feedback on your website through reviews.

The success of a product depends on more than utility and usability alone. Products which are usable, useful, findable, credible, desirable, accessible, and valuable are much more likely to succeed in the marketplace. We have successfully discussed the seven factors that play a crucial role in deciding the total effectiveness and efficiency of the design's user experience. A designer can take his designs to new heights by following these critical factors, ultimately improving the user experience. The better the user experience, the popular the product or website becomes within its users.

Go through these factors to understand the core concept and develop your business. Adopt these seven factors explained above and enhance the user experience of your brand successfully.

UX management is a challenging role, but if you can build an effective team of UX professionals and set up the right work environment for them to thrive in, it will make your job much easier.

Lead by integrating these UX management strategies into your UX design projects:

-Give constructive feedback when needed; show them how valuable their contributions are (even if it is not seen externally).

-Let teammates know what's expected from them on projects

-Provide opportunities for growth within the company or design firm

-Offer encouragement during tough times—or even easier tasks like giving praise for completing an easy task quickly!

Make sure everyone on staff has an understanding of what their role entails within the company/organization as well as how it contributes to meeting organizational goals. Be clear about expectations on projects, provide opportunities for growth within the company, and take advantage of collaborative work structures. This all will tell your team that you are serious about the quality of work they put out.

Finally, get their input on how to continue improving the UX culture within the organization.

Always remember to create alignment as a UX manager. There are many different ways that you can do this, but the most important thing is that you make sure your team understands everything from the company's values and goals to their roles in meeting those objectives.

Even if you are already familiar with what needs to be done (and everyone else is too), communicate the vision anyway. This will ensure that there are no misunderstandings and encourage your team to do their best work.

Regularly check in with your UX team to make sure they are happy working at your company/organization and ask if they have any suggestions for how to improve things.

A happy team is a productive team. You will have a lot more success in creating a UX Culture when you have clear priorities that are communicated to everyone from the company's values and goals to their roles in meeting those objectives.

Remember that communicating with your UX team is important and ensure you set up a culture of continuous feedback. This will help your team stay on track with expectations and provide you with great suggestions for how to improve your UX culture.

As a UX manager, it's important to keep in mind that running a UX team is not just about the work that gets done; it's about how your UX designers and researchers feel as they go through the process.

Always ensure you are helping your team grow and ensure you stay on track with creating career paths within the UX world and your team becomes more than just UX designers. If you follow these guidelines and consistently strive to improve UX within your company, you will be on the way to building a successful UX team and will be on your way to UX management.

Set precedents and ensure you are following the best way to move forward in your new position as a UX manager. Ensure you set your precedents by being clear with everyone on your team and being consistent with the work you are doing. Always ensure that you are maintaining alignment across all levels of the design team.

This will ensure that you are creating the best UX possible to meet end goals for your organization. We went over the most common fears for managing a UX team and overcoming these obstacles. Ensure you stay on track by keeping the lines of communication open.

The Q&A section next will address some of the commonly asked questions about UX management.

Thank you for taking the time to read this book. I hope that it will be a useful resource, both now and in the future, as you work on managing your UX team.

If you have any other questions, comments or suggestions for this book, feel free to message me on Instagram @jonbinderrr

I hope that this book has been useful for you and please consider leaving a review on Amazon to help other people find this book. This book was a lot of work to create and I would greatly appreciate it.

May you live long and design great user experiences.

Q&A SECTION

The following is a list of answers to some commonly asked questions about UX management.

1) How do I get a job as a UX Manager?

The best way to find a job as a UX manager is to do a lot of online research and networking on LinkedIn. One way to find jobs in UX management is by setting up an automated alert for job postings that use various keywords, such as "UX" or "UX Manager" or "User Experience". Personally, I like the websites Indeed.com and LinkedIn for finding the best UX job postings.

Keep an eye out for interesting job opportunities and begin your search with these suggestions. The work of UX managers can range from managing large companies, overseeing multiple projects at the same time, creating new programs internally or externally, or taking a more limited role in guiding UX strategy. Considering all of this when looking for a position ensures the best possible fit if you decide it's what you want to do.

UX managers typically have a very diverse range of skills, so it might be difficult for potential employers to understand who you are specifically and what your value is unless they get to know you personally. Going out there and doing things that interest you will put you in the right position - after all, people like to hire people who do things they like.

2) How do I deal with difficult UX team members?

The best way to deal with difficult UX team members is to try and find out why they are difficult and use that information against them (in a good way). For example, if someone has trouble communicating their thoughts, UX managers can help by giving them more time to process things. The same goes for people who have trouble coming up with design ideas on their own- UX managers might want to give them more time to explore their creativity. Being lenient in these circumstances does wonders.

3) How do I measure UX success?

The best way to measure the success of your UX activities is to establish methods for recording usability metrics. UX managers should be able to learn how users use the UX and what they like and dislike about it. Using this information, UX managers can then set up ways for recording these metrics in order to monitor their progress over time.

4) How do the roles and responsibilities compare between UX Designers vs. UX Researchers vs. UX Writers?

The first thing to understand is that UX Designers, UX Researchers and UX Writers are all very different roles and require different skill sets and talents to master.

UX designers have a creative and artistic role in designing and producing wireframes, mockups, prototypes and other deliverables required by the project.

UX Designers need to be able to work closely with Product Managers and stakeholders in order to understand what look and feel they want from an experience.

Most UX designers have a strong sense of the unspoken "rules" of design and can see what looks great and which designs are lacking. They can work with wireframes and prototypes to create rough mockups and visuals.

What separates good UX designers from great UX Designers is attention to detail, an eye for design, and the ability to spot inconsistencies in designs. Great UX Designers will also be able to inform you if different design ideas are technically feasible or not. UX designers can be expected to have a strong sense of user interface design and the ability to sketch, storyboard or wireframe their ideas before fleshing them out into full-fledged mockups.

After completing rough sketches and prototypes, good UX designers should feel comfortable creating high-fidelity mock-ups. I'm not necessarily talking about full-fledged Pixel Perfect prototypes, but rather what I'm talking about is quality designs that you can present to stakeholders and Leadership.

UX Researchers on the other hand are specialists who conduct tests and methods to understand their users' behaviors, needs, and motivations. They provide real data, insights, and recommendations for improving the overall user experience.

Researchers are great at synthesizing research data into stories that can be communicated effectively to UX Designers, Product Managers, or other stakeholders. They can determine what research is needed and determine which testing methodologies would be the most effective at each of the different phases of the development lifecycle.

UX Researchers are also responsible for summarizing, organizing, and reporting on data after conducting any necessary usability tests.

A great example of how best to think about what UX researchers can do for your team can be summarized with the story of the Toyota Motor Company. Toyota was producing a car that was failing in Europe but was very successful in Japan. The Corolla was failing in Europe because it featured a high-revving and powerful engine, which works fine for cars in Japan but not so much for folks using their cars to drive on small roads and the ancient cities in Europe.

So Toyota's UX team did some research and found that their users in Europe valued smaller, engines with better fuel economy over horsepower. So they started putting smaller engines in the car and using a multi-speed transmission to get the same power without having an engine with 8 cylinders. And it worked! Sales of the Corolla went up by over 30% the next year all because of UX Research and understanding what their users valued. They valued gas mileage and fuel economy and the Japanese leadership team at Toyota only learned this through UX research and talking to their users in Europe.

UX researchers help you understand your users' behaviors, motivations, and expectations.

UX Research is the work of observing and interviewing users to uncover their motivations for doing what they do. This research provides insights into how your customers experience your product or service. UX research enables us to know our users better than they know themselves.

UX research is the process of understanding how people experience your organization's "touchpoints" and what can be done to improve them or make them more valuable for the user.

Do you have a website? That's a touchpoint.

Do you have an automated voicemail message recording? That's a touchpoint.

Do you send out any emails or auto-generated messages? That's a touchpoint.

Do you interact with your customers on social media? That's definitely a touchpoint.

UX Researchers gather information about how people experience your touchpoints by using a variety of different methods like surveys, interviews, contextual inquiries, diary studies, and more, to gather information about the user-product interaction and to understand people's motivations for doing what they do.

More on this in later chapters where we will outline all of the most important XU Research methods and talk about when each method should be used at the different stages in the product development lifecycle.

UX Writers on the other hand work closely with UX designers and UX researchers to create text and documentation for screen designs, user stories, training manuals, and any other extra text required by the project.

They write crisp and clear copy that users can understand without adding extra fluff or unnecessary verbiage. UX writers are also responsible for ensuring that the voice of the business is reflected in all copy, regardless of whether it is formal marketing-speak or casual chatty vernacular. Whatever the voice or tone of the organization is, it should remain consistent.

The best way to think about what UX Writers can do for your team is like this: Your users don't interact with your company's UX team. They interact with very specific parts of your product or service. As a user read the text or actual copy, they hear it as if someone was speaking to them and they expect to be treated with respect and have clear information provided to them. Nearly all of your organization's touchpoints are accompanied by text that has to be written by someone.

UX Researchers collect information from users about what they need and UX Writers translate that information into words that everyone can understand. UX Designers then work to present those words in a style that is consistent and pleasing to read.

UX writers bridge the gap between what we need to communicate about our user experience and how best to communicate it to our team members, stakeholders, or other interested parties.

UX Writers are not just translators of words! They have a set of skills that can be applied to any situation when words need to be crafted for users.

UX Researchers are often involved in the writing process to help communicate in a way that is concise and easy to understand, but UX Writers also use their knowledge of UX concepts in addition to whatever research has been conducted.

Different people have different skillsets, so it's important to place your team member in an environment where they can play to their strengths.

5) What do UX team members need to perform well?

UX team members need clear expectations, UX design, and research tools, and for UX managers to be accessible, approachable, and supportive. UX managers should provide opportunities for employees to learn new skills by attending workshops and conferences. They should also encourage their employees to take on challenging tasks as this helps the UX team member grow professionally.

6) What kind of work environment does a UX team need?

Your UX team needs an environment that is calm, serene, and quiet. If possible, UX managers should have a separate workstation where they are not distracted by the hustle-and-bustle of everyday office activity. Reduced noise levels will make it easier for UX managers to focus on their projects without anyone disturbing them. Fun objects like toys and books create a playful and informal atmosphere that contributes to creativity and happy employees.

7) How do UX managers avoid office politics?

UX managers should not get involved in office politics by either taking sides in an argument or openly criticize anyone if they are not present to defend themselves. UX managers should be able to listen and work around the situation without choosing sides. This will allow for future opportunities like passing on feedback to others so they do not make the same mistakes again - ultimately promoting a positive and productive environment for you and your staff.

8) How can I ensure that my UX team is productive?

UX managers can ensure that their UX team is productive by keeping them accountable for their actions and projects. UX managers should also be prepared to reward employees for a job well done, even if it's as simple as giving out a compliment. Being generous with praise is always a good way to get the best out of employees.

9) How do I align UX with the business strategy?

The best way to align your UX with the business strategy is to put yourself in your customer's shoes and imagine how their experience relates to the overall goals of the organization. UX managers should always be on the lookout for changes or improvements to the experience that alight with key metrics or objectives and key results of their organization.

10) What are some great UX blogs or Resources?

Some great UX blogs include UX Magazine, Nielsen Norman Group, and UX Matters. Some good podcasts about UX are UX Movement, UX Podcast, and Usability Geek.

11) Can you go into more detail about some of the job responsibilities of a UX Writer and What is UX writing?

UX Writers on the other hand are specialists who communicate UX concepts in a variety of mediums, writing copy for user-testing tasks, writing personas and scenarios to help UX Designers understand user motivations, editing wireframes, prototypes or final designs to make them more easily understood by customers, and changing and editing text to make sure users understand what actions to take.

UX writing is an undervalued aspect of user experience design, but can significantly improve customer satisfaction. As such, it deserves as much focus as other areas of UX design such as visual design or usability testing.

You might be tempted to think that UX writing only covers product copy — things like software error messages, website terms and conditions pages, and app onboarding text — but in reality, UX writers also contribute content to research reports, data sheets, and marketing materials.

UX writers work closely with designers and product managers throughout a project's life cycle to ensure their content is in line with the UX design

UX writing is one of those things that not many people notice, but they would miss it if it weren't there. Having a well-crafted user experience is all about ensuring the right information is communicated to the right person at the right time, which sounds simple enough. However, it requires good design as well as clear and concise content. UX writing covers those aspects of UX design that are not purely visual or usability-related.

In this article, we'll look at what UX writing means for your product, how it can impact the user's experience, and why you need UX writers on your team. We'll also discuss how to get started and get a job as a UX writer.

While most people wouldn't think to include UX writing in their definition of UX, we're here to tell you that UX writing contributes to great user experience — and, therefore, great user feelings about your product.

UX Writing is content that contributes to great user experiences by being clear and concise. UX writers help designers and product managers communicate their products to the right people at the right time. UX writing is one of those things that tend to be undervalued but would be missed if it weren't there.

Having a clear, concise user experience can seem like an easy enough thing to write about — but requires good design as well as the content. UX writing covers aspects of UX design not purely visual or usability related.

UX writing includes things like product copy, research reports, data sheets, and marketing materials.

UX writers work closely with designers and product managers throughout the project life cycle to ensure they are meeting the needs of the user with their content.

Startups need UX writers just as much as more established companies do — but there aren't many jobs available for it yet! To be a great UX writer you should have excellent communication skills, attention to detail, and an eye for what works best in the context of your client's brand.

At this point, you may be wondering how to become skilled at UX writing if it is such an underexplored field. The answer is simple: start practicing! Read through product content and see how it sounds. See what works, what doesn't work, and what could be improved. If you have colleagues or friends working in UX design, try your hand at editing their work as well.

Be concise

Be concise in all your writing. Don't use words if they can be replaced with fewer, more effective ones. For example, "several people" could become "many people" or even simply "people." Remember that your goal is to carry the message of your design in the clearest way possible.

Avoid long blocks of text

Long blocks of text are difficult to read on small screens. When you're dealing with long chunks of information, it's far better to break them up into smaller paragraphs and use tools like bullet points or lists where possible. Spaces can also be used effectively in some cases — for example, when summarizing the content of a page that shows all the steps necessary to complete an action.

Avoid double negatives

Double negatives are hard to read and increase cognitive load — they make users spend extra time thinking about what the message means. It's best to not include double negatives whenever possible.

When using a product, users aren't immersed in the user interface itself but in their work. Consequently, users don't read UI text — they scan it. Help them scan the text by writing it in short, scannable blocks. Chunk text into shorter sentences and paragraphs. Keep the most important text upfront and then ruthlessly edit what comes after it.

Use specific verbs whenever possible

Specific verbs are more meaningful to users than abstract ones. For example, "connect" is more specific than "link," and both are preferable to "share."

UX writing isn't all about following rules — it's about balancing the needs of your client with the needs of your end-user. UX writers should focus on

Specific verbs (such as connect or save) are more meaningful to users than generic ones (such as configure or manage).

Make the Copy Consistent

Inconsistency creates confusion. One typical example of inconsistency is replacing a word with a synonym in a different part of the UI. For instance, if you decide to call the process of arranging something "Scheduling" in one part of UI do not call it a "Booking" in other parts of your UI.

Avoid Jargon

One of the significant characteristics of effective UX writing is clarity and simplicity. For clarity, you need to remove the technical terms and use familiar, understandable words and phrases instead. It's especially important to avoid jargon in error messages.

Don't: System error (code #2234): An authentication error has occurred
Do: Sign-in error: You entered an incorrect password

Write in the present tense

Avoid using the future tense to describe the action.
Don't: Video has been downloaded

Do: Video downloaded

Write in the active voice

The passive voice makes readers yawn. Compare this
sentence in both voices:
Don't: The Search button should be clicked when you are ready
to search for an item.
Do: Click the Search button to search for an article.

Use numerals

Use numerals in place of words for numbers.
Don't: You have two missed calls
Do: You have 2 missed calls

Avoid showing all details upfront

Sometimes it might be helpful to provide additional information
or supplemental instruction for users. But all too often such
details are presented upfront. Too much information can
quickly overwhelm users. Thus, reveal detail as needed. Use a
mechanism of progressive disclosure to show more details. In
the most basic form, this mechanism can be implemented as a
'Read more' link to the full content.

Evernote uses progressive disclosure to provide more
information about the benefit.

Progressive disclosure is especially good for mobile UI (where
designers have a limited screen space to work with).

Identify interactive elements appropriately

Users don't like surprises. They hate situations when they're expecting one thing, and end up with another. People should be able to tell at a glance what an element does.

Choose labels that communicate and differentiate what the object does.

When labeling buttons and other interactive elements, use action verbs, such as 'Connect,' 'Send,' 'Subscribe' instead of vague 'Okay' or 'Submit.'

Be careful when using humor

A lot of designers say that incorporating humor in UI makes it sound more human. But similar to any other component of UI, humor should be designed. People are likely to read the text in your interface many times, and what might seem clever at first can become irritating over time (especially if you use humor in error messages). Also, remember that humor in one culture doesn't necessarily translate well to other cultures.

Use language that's consistent with the user's platform

The terms we use when describing interaction with a desktop app do not necessarily apply to mobile platforms. For example, if you design an iPhone app, we can't say 'click' when referring to the action. We need to say 'tap' instead.

Use 'today,' 'yesterday' or 'tomorrow' instead of a date

People don't use the date when they refer to the day before the present day. They say 'yesterday.' The same principle can be applied to UIs. Instead of giving a date, say 'today,' 'yesterday' or 'tomorrow.' It prevents users from using the calendar each time they want to know when the event happened. But remember that these terms can be confusing or inaccurate if you don't account for the current locale.

Use graphics if they will help you communicate

Human beings are incredibly visual creatures. An ability to interpret visual information is hard-wired into our brains. In some contexts, it might be nearly impossible to say something in words. That's where imagery can support us and make text comprehensible. Below is an example that helps users to find specific information.

When writing, it's important to make sure you clearly define your target audience and meet their needs. In some cases, you may be writing for a very specific user type or role that will read only one page on your website—so it's important to get that experience just right!

In the end, UX writing is a crucial element of a clear, concise, and effective user experience — which is what every company wants. So if you've been considering adding a UX writer to your list of roles, please do so!

Key Takeaways UX writing is an important aspect of great user experiences that isn't purely visual or usability-related. UX writers help designers and product managers communicate their products by being clear and concise.

Start practicing UX writing by reading through product content, editing your colleagues' work, learning from mentors, learning about common mistakes others have made. Avoid double negatives in all your writing. By using bullet points or lists where possible, making use of spaces when summarizing the steps necessary to complete an action, and be mindful of the words you are choosing to include. Always write with the clearest message possible in mind.

In my experience, if your budget is limited or you can only hire 1 UX role, it's a smart idea to hire UX Designers with an eye towards the potential for becoming UX Researchers. This is because most people can learn to communicate and synthesize research data, but there are a limited number of people who have the talent and creativity required to produce wireframes, mockups, or other design deliverables.

It's also very useful for UX Designers to speak the language of engineering and software development, as this makes it easier for them to work more closely on teams with UX Researchers or Developers. When interviewing designers and researchers make sure to check that they have a history of working on development teams and translating user requirements into actionable recommendations for the development team.

To hire the best people in UX, you need to be prepared to kiss a lot of frogs before you meet your prince. By this I mean don't be afraid to conduct a lot of job interviews to find the right candidate. The more people you talk to and the more effort you put into interviewing them, the more likely you'll hire a good UX worker. In my experience, there is a direct correlation between the quality of UX team members you end up hiring and how much effort you put into the hiring process. Take your time and do the necessary work to find the right person, trust me, and Steve that it'll pay off in the end.

What are the skills necessary for a successful UX Manager

The work of UX managers varies from company to company and it's important to know the scope of the position before applying for it. UX managers often need to have skills in both technical and interpersonal fields, such as user-centered design, project management, UI engineering, data analysis or approvals procedures as well as knowledge of information security issues and other IT areas.

UX managers typically manage a large team or project themselves with few direct reports. It is key for this type of person to produce meaningful results through persuasion by presenting solutions that represent a variety of perspectives - theirs included - not simply orders from above. Other requirements include managing budgets responsibly and actively pursuing opportunities related to the product or service

Designing an environment that is conducive to creativity and productivity in your team's workspace

Designing an environment in which your team can feel engaged, stimulated, and productive is key for a successful UX workplace.

There are important principles to follow when creating this workspace. Firstly, be motivated by the idea of constant change - coming up with fresh new ideas to help improve projects for your company's customers is crucial. New design practices are constantly emerging with potential for expanding what might have been thought of as standard procedure.

The most important rule in regards to designing an environment that engages the UX team is creating a product roadmap that moves forward by following these natural sparks of creativity and growth.

Tips on maintaining relationships with clients, stakeholders, and other members of the organization or company you work for.

- Respecting your clients when you're brainstorming ideas.
- It's important to understand what's going on in their mind and to do your be UX strategies for a project. To do this, you must be good at listening and ge about the person in front of you.
- Respecting your stakeholders and fellow employees by treating them fairly
- Don't forget that it's not always about you and your thoughts - sometimes c be worth exploring.
- Taking care of your team by maintaining a work-life balance (within reason
- Practicing self-care is crucial for an engaged UX professional who is lookir

Why is it important for UX people to always keep learning about design trends, processes, new technologies, and so on?

Just like UX managers must keep up with industry changes to do this job well, the same goes for their staff. The UX team needs to be up to date on the latest design techniques and processes to help them do their job well.

They also need fresh new ideas and tools with which to approach new challenges. If they aren't up to date on current trends in the field, then their work will quickly become obsolete due to competitors who are up to date on current trends.

Thank you for reading UX management methods. If you found this content helpful, then please consider leaving an online review so that other people know how awesome this book is.

I hope that you found it helpful. Please consider reading some other books in our series like UX Research Methods and UX Design Methods.

If you would like to get in touch or just reach out and say what's up, then connect with me on Instagram at @jonbinderrr

I would love to hear from you.

www.ingramcontent.com/pod-product-compliance
Lightning Source LLC
Chambersburg PA
CBHW052140070326
40690CB00047B/1250